P9-ASH-293

THE CASE FOR
Miracles

• STUDENT EDITION •

Also by Lee Strobel

THE CASE FOR
Miracles

• STUDENT EDITION •

*A Journalist Explores the Evidence
for the Supernatural*

New York Times Bestselling author
LEE STROBEL

with Jane Vogel

ZONDERVAN

The Case for Miracles Student Edition
Copyright © 2018 by Lee Strobel

This title is also available as a Zondervan ebook.

Requests for information should be addressed to:
Zondervan, *3900 Sparks Dr. SE, Grand Rapids, Michigan 49546*

ISBN 978-0-310-74636-2 (softcover)

ISBN 978-0-310-74723-9 (ebook)

All Scripture quotations, unless otherwise noted, are taken from the Holy Bible, New International Version®, NIV®. Copyright © 1973, 1978, 1984, 2011 by Biblica, Inc.® Used by permission of Zondervan. All rights reserved worldwide. www.Zondervan.com. The "NIV" and "New International Version" are trademarks registered in the United States Patent and Trademark Office by Biblica, Inc.®

Any Internet addresses (websites, blogs, etc.) and telephone numbers in this book are offered as a resource. They are not intended in any way to be or imply an endorsement by Zondervan, nor does Zondervan vouch for the content of these sites and numbers for the life of this book.

All rights reserved. No part of this publication may be reproduced, stored in a retrieval system, or transmitted in any form or by any means—electronic, mechanical, photocopy, recording, or any other—except for brief quotations in printed reviews, without the prior permission of the publisher.

Interior design: Denise Froehlich and Kait Lamphere

Printed in the United States of America

18 19 20 21 22 23 / LSC / 15 14 13 12 11 10 9 8 7 6 5 4 3 2 1

R0451623279

CONTENTS

•———•

INVESTIGATING THE MIRACULOUS

Everyone had high hopes for Ben. He finished third in his high school class and got the highest SAT score of any student in twenty years from a Detroit public school.

He could only afford the ten-dollar admission fee to apply to one college, so he chose Yale University and got a full scholarship. He thought he was pretty hot stuff—until the end of his first semester.

Ben's dream was to become a doctor—but he was failing chemistry, a course he needed to pass if he wanted to get into med school. His only hope was to ace the final exam. But he wasn't ready for it, not by a long shot.

That evening, he prayed. "Lord, medicine is the only thing I ever wanted to do," he said. "Would you please tell me what it is *you* really want me to do?"

He planned to study for the exam all night, but

despite his best intentions, he fell asleep. All seemed lost—until he had a dream: he was alone in an auditorium, where a shadowy figure began writing chemistry problems on the chalkboard.

"When I went to take the test the next morning, it was like the *Twilight Zone*. I recognized the first problem as one I had dreamed about," Ben recalls. "And the next, and the next, and the next. I aced the exam and got a good grade in chemistry. And I promised the Lord he would never have to do that for me again!"

Ben went on to achieve his goal of becoming a doctor. By age thirty-three, he was the youngest director of pediatric neurosurgery in the country, performing pioneering operations at Johns Hopkins Hospital. He separated twins conjoined at the brain, performed the first successful neurosurgery on a fetus, developed new methods of treating brain stem and spinal cord tumors, and was awarded the nation's highest civilian honor, the Presidential Medal of Freedom.

A 2014 poll ranked Benjamin Solomon Carson Sr. as among the ten most admired people in America. He was even a potential candidate to become president of the United States. All because a dream helped him pass a chemistry course nearly fifty years ago.[1]

What do you think? Was this a coincidence? A tall tale exaggerated to promote a political career? Or a miraculous intervention by God?

In rural Africa, far from pharmacies and hospitals, a woman died in childbirth, leaving behind a two-year-old daughter and a premature baby. With no incubator, no electricity, and few supplies, the newborn's life was in danger.

A helper filled a hot water bottle to help the baby stay warm, but suddenly the bottle burst—and it was the last hot water bottle in the village.

The doctor, a missionary named Helen Roseveare, asked the villagers to pray for the situation—but a faith-filled ten-year-old named Ruth seemed to go too far.

"Please God, send us a water bottle," she begged. "It'll be no good tomorrow, God; the baby will be dead. So please send it this afternoon." And then she added, "And while you are about it, would you please send a dolly for the little girl so she'll know you really love her?"

Dr. Roseveare wasn't sure how to respond. "I was put on the spot," she says. "Could I honestly say, 'Amen'? I just did not believe that God could do this. Oh, yes, I know that he can do everything. The Bible says so. But there are limits, aren't there?"

The only hope of getting a water bottle would be if someone sent one in a care package. But Dr. Roseveare had never received any packages during the almost four years she had lived there. "Anyway," she thought, "if anyone did send a package, who would put in a hot water bottle? I live on the equator!"

A couple of hours later, a car dropped off a twenty-two-pound package. Dr. Roseveare opened it and sorted through the contents: some clothing for the orphans in the village, bandages for the leprosy patients, and a bit of food.

Oh, and this: "As I put my hand in again, I felt the . . . could it really be? I grasped it, and pulled it out. Yes. A brand-new water bottle!" says Roseveare. "I cried. I had not asked God to send it; I had not truly believed that he could."

With that, little Ruth rushed forward. "If God has sent the bottle, he must have sent the dolly too!" she exclaimed.

She dug through the packaging and found it at the bottom of the parcel: a beautifully dressed doll. Ruth said, "Here's the dolly for that little girl, so she'll know that Jesus really loves her."

That care package had been packed *five months earlier* by Roseveare's former Sunday school class. The leader, feeling prompted by God, included the hot water bottle; a girl contributed the doll. And this package, the only one ever to arrive, was delivered the same day Ruth prayed for it with the faith of a child.[2]

A mere twist of fate? An exaggerated story? Or perhaps a miracle?

―――――――

Lynn Groesbeck, a twenty-five-year-old single mother studying to become a medical assistant, was driving home on a darkened Utah highway in 2015 when her car suddenly struck a cement barrier and veered off the road.

The red Dodge sedan landed upside down, partially submerged in the icy waters of a river and not visible from the roadway.

Fourteen hours later, a fisherman spotted the wreck and called the police. When four officers arrived, they spotted an arm through the car's window, but it seemed unlikely that anyone could have survived such a horrific accident.

That's when they heard a woman's voice softly calling out, "Help me! We're in here!" The words were as clear as day. An officer shouted back, "Hang in there! We're trying!"

The officers plunged into the near-freezing waters, which at times reached their necks, and used their collective strength to pull the car onto its side.

What they discovered shocked them. Lynn had been killed on impact. But in the backseat, they found an unconscious eighteen-month-old girl, who had hung upside down, attached by her car seat, throughout the freezing night, the top of her blond hair just inches from the water.

The rescuers formed a human chain to bring the child to safety. The little girl was briefly hospitalized and later released in good health.

But that voice—where had it come from? Not from Lynn, who was already dead. Not from the child, who was unconscious—besides, said a rescuer, it was unquestionably the voice of a woman.

Officer Tyler Beddoes said he wouldn't have believed what happened if the other rescuers hadn't heard the voice too. "That's the part that really sends me for a whirl," he told reporters. "I'm not a typically religious guy. It's hard to explain—it was definitely something. Where and why it came from, I'm not sure."

Many people didn't hesitate to call it a miracle. But could there be another explanation? Perhaps rescuers mistook the sound of a breeze through the trees. Or maybe the mother somehow momentarily regained life at just the right instant to give the police the extra adrenaline they needed. Or possibly it was a product of the overactive imagination of the officers, whose senses were heightened in the crisis.

A miracle? Officer Beddoes isn't sure, but given the circumstances, even this skeptical cop conceded: "That's what you think of."[3]

———————

There are more than a thousand people in the British auditorium. The lights are bright, and the organ music swells with old-time gospel music. The healing evangelist speaks in an unknown tongue; he casts out demons; he touches people on the face and they instantly fall backward. There is an unmistakable sense of excitement and anticipation in the room.

The evangelist, who seems to be responding to some private word of knowledge, begins calling out diseases that are being healed. Soon, people line up to testify that their ailments have miraculously disappeared. Someone says his short-sightedness is cured. Another reports that a persistent ringing in her ears has stopped. A third says his sprained ankle has suddenly been restored to full strength and he can walk again without pain.

The evening has the feel of a charismatic healing service, but with one major difference: the "healing evangelist" is an atheist.

Darren Brown is a former Christian who is now one of England's most famous illusionists. "It is his ability as a 'mentalist' that sets him apart," says Christian commentator Justin Brierley. "Using a mixture of suggestion, 'cold reading,' hypnosis, and plain old trickery, Brown has the ability to make people believe in God, miracles, and the power of prayer."

In his stage show *Miracles*, Brown produces an exciting

and stimulating atmosphere. "If I can create some type of adrenaline rush, then someone with a bad back is going to tell me that they can't feel the pain," he explains. "That's a chemical thing."

What's more, he adds, "They would also hit the floor when I touched them on the face because they have a certain expectation. When you go to these events as a believer you know what's supposed to happen. So I show clips of people doing that. By the time they come up on stage, there's a similar expectation of what they're supposed to do."

Do these "fake miracles" discredit other miracle claims? Or because this atmosphere doesn't resemble how most healings take place, is Brown's show irrelevant to the question of whether some miracles are actually genuine?

———

I'm the kind of person who likes to have evidence. I have degrees in journalism and in law, and I was an investigative newspaper reporter for fourteen years. So, yeah—you could say I tend to be skeptical. And yet, ironically, it was my skepticism that ultimately drove me to faith in Jesus.

You see, my wife, Leslie, became a Christian after we were married. That's when I decided to investigate the case against Christianity. I was sure that the evidence would end up disproving the entire religion, and I would rescue Leslie from this "cult."

To my dismay, the data of science convinced me there was a supernatural Creator, while the evidence from history proved to me that Jesus of Nazareth was resurrected from the dead, confirming his identity as the unique Son of God.

The undeniable conclusion that Christianity is true prompted me to put my trust in Christ. Later, I left my newspaper career to spend my life telling others the good news about Jesus.

However, my skeptical nature didn't entirely disappear. Did I believe in miracles? Yes, of course. I was convinced that the resurrection and other miracles occurred as the Gospels reported. But that left open the question of whether God is still in the miracle business today.

In other words, does a miracle-performing God actually exist, and has he left his fingerprints all over supernatural events through history down to the present age? Is he even available to intervene in *your* life today?

That's what I set out to determine in writing this book. In the end, I'll ask you for your own verdict.

PART 1

Do Miracles REALLY HAPPEN?

CHAPTER 1

• — •

WHAT ABOUT SCIENCE?

Marguerite was a small girl when she developed an open sore at the corner of her left eye. Despite ongoing treatment, the sore continued to worsen, to the point it began to eat away at her bones on the inside of her nose and the roof of her mouth. She lost her sense of smell and had trouble eating, sleeping, and even breathing. The odor from the sore was so repulsive that Marguerite was kept away from other children. Her condition was considered hopeless.

Then one day, after years of suffering, while Marguerite was praying with others in a chapel, she was completely healed. Even the evidence of bone deterioration vanished immediately. Medical and eyewitness evidence verified the healing. In the following months, eighty other miracle claims followed.

But one man insisted that the healings were not miraculous.[4]

Oh—and this happened in 1656.

The Laws of Nature

Why do I tell you a story about one man's word against many, several hundred years ago? Because the man was a philosopher named David Hume, and his work is still influential today—not just in philosophy, but in science.

Here's a quick overview of what Hume said about miracles:

1. A miracle is something that breaks the laws of nature.
2. The laws of nature can't be broken.
3. Therefore, miracles do not exist.

A quick Google search on "science and miracles" showed me that this view is still common. Here's what one professor of physics says about the prevalent view today:

"All explanation in modern science rests ultimately on the assumption that nature follows 'universal laws,' that is, laws that apply in all time, places, and circumstances throughout the universe." (Follow that? It's basically Hume's point 2, above.)

The professor continues: "But many of the miracles in which religious people believe would certainly violate the laws of physics." (That's what Hume says in point 1.)

"It is this that leads some to conclude that miracles are, quite simply, impossible." (Hume's point 3.)[5]

So what does that mean? Do you have to reject science in order to believe that miracles can happen?

Interrupted, Not Broken

Here's the best example I've heard. Imagine I'm holding a pen. If I drop it, the law of gravity tells me it will fall to the floor. But if I were to reach out and grab the pen in midair, I wouldn't be breaking the law of gravity; I would merely be intervening. And certainly, if God exists, he would have the ability to intervene in the world that he himself created.

Instead of saying that miracles *break* the laws of nature, it would be better to say that a miracle is a *temporary exception* to the ordinary course of nature.

Is that unscientific? Some people would say so. A friend of mine told me the story of talking with his professor about miracles. The professor dismissed every bit of evidence my friend gave. Finally, my friend asked him, 'If somebody were raised from the dead in front of you, would you believe it?'"

The professor answered, "No."

In my opinion, that's bad science. The professor was unwilling to consider the evidence because he had already decided in advance that miracles were impossible. If you insist that miracles have a zero chance of ever happening, as this professor did, then you're not going to find any. But if you keep an open mind and follow the evidence wherever it leads—well, it might take you to unexpected places.

A Scientific Study of Miracles

Dr. Michael Shermer is probably the most famous doubter in the United States, and even founded and edits a magazine called *Skeptic*. I knew he didn't believe in anything supernatural—not God and certainly not miracles. I wanted to hear what he had to say on the subject, so I went to talk with him in his office in Los Angeles.

As he and I spoke, it was clear to me that Dr. Shermer wasn't skeptical about everything in this world. So I asked, "How do you define *skeptic*?"

"It's taking a scientific approach to claims. The burden of proof should be on the claimant. The Food and Drug Administration doesn't approve a drug just because you say it works. The burden of proof isn't on them; *you* have to prove your drug works. And it should be like that with all claims."

I asked Shermer whether he agreed with scientist Jerry Coyne of the University of Chicago, an atheist who said,

"It would be a close-minded scientist who would say that miracles are impossible in principle." Coyne added that "to have real confidence in a miracle, one needs evidence—massive, well-documented, and either replicated or independently corroborated evidence from multiple and reliable sources." His conclusion: "No religious miracle even comes close to meeting those standards."[6]

"I'd tend to agree," Shermer replied. "I doubt if there's something supernatural, outside of space and time, that intervenes in our world. But if there were, we would be able to measure its effects. And if it reaches into our environment, then it's part of the natural world, not supernatural."

"So," I said, "you wouldn't be opposed to an investigation of seemingly miraculous events?"

"Not at all. Let's check them out as best we can. Let's test them. Bring on the evidence. As Coyne said, we can't rule them out in principle, but I don't think there's sufficient proof of anything miraculous."

Dr. Shermer went on to say that the problem with stories about healings and other miracles is that they're just that—stories. "We need to study them scientifically. And when we do, guess what? Science doesn't support them. I'm sure you're familiar with STEP."

The Study of the Therapeutic Effects of Intercessory Prayer (STEP) was a ten-year, $2.4 million clinical trial of the effects of prayer on 1,802 cardiac bypass patients at six hospitals.

Patients having cardiac bypass surgery were broken into three groups. One group was prayed for and a second group was not, although nobody in either group knew for sure whether they were being uplifted in prayer. A third group was prayed for after being told they definitely would receive prayer. Then researchers tracked the number of complications from the surgeries.

"The results were very revealing," said Shermer. "There was no difference in the rate of complications for patients who were prayed for and those who were not. Nothing. Zero. And, in fact, those who knew they were being prayed for had *more* complications. This is the best prayer study we have. So when you get beyond anecdotes and use the scientific method, there's no evidence for the miraculous.

"That's not good for your side, Lee."

Studying the Study

Did the STEP study really establish, as Dr. Shermer suggested, that when scientific analysis is applied, there is no persuasive evidence for the miraculous?

That was the question prompting my journey to the campus of Indiana University in Bloomington. I checked my watch as I drove my rental car. Still plenty of time to make my appointment with a scholar who is figuring out ways to use science to investigate faith.

Candy Gunther Brown is a professor of religious studies at Indiana University. "I do not assume the existence or nonexistence of a deity or other suprahuman force," she explains. "What I argue is that people's religious beliefs often have real-world effects that can be studied [scientifically]."[7]

What brought me to Indiana was her focus on studying the impact of prayer on healing.

Does Prayer Make a Difference?

I asked Dr. Brown for her opinion of the STEP project that Dr. Shermer had cited as having shown no impact—or even a slightly harmful effect—on recovering cardiac patients. I expected it would be a rather routine conversation, but frankly I ended up thoroughly surprised—even stunned—by what she said.

"Let me start by saying that there have been 'gold standard' studies before and after STEP that reached the opposite conclusion: that the group receiving prayer had *better* outcomes," she said, and described two of them.

Now I was confused. "Then why do you think STEP reached such a different conclusion?" I asked.

"That's where things get very intriguing," she said.

"If you're going to study prayer, wouldn't it be important who was praying, who they were praying to, and how they were praying?"

That seemed obvious. "Of course," I replied.

"In one of the studies, the people praying were 'born again' Protestants and Catholics, who were active in daily devotional prayer and in fellowship with a local church. They were praying to the 'Judeo-Christian God.'"

That made sense to me. As born-again believers, they would have faith in a personal God who is loving and who possesses the power and inclination to supernaturally intervene in people's lives.

"In another study, the intercessors were required to believe in a personal God who hears and answers prayers made on behalf of the sick."

Again, that seemed entirely appropriate. "What about STEP, which found no beneficial effects of prayer?" I asked.

"Here's where the difference comes in. The only Protestants recruited to participate in the study were from Silent Unity. Unity's leaders have long denied that prayer works miracles and have even called petitionary prayers 'useless,'"[8] Dr. Brown answered.

The group instead practices what it calls "affirmative prayer." Affirmative prayer involves repeating positive statements, such as, "We are imbued with divinity and are physically healthy." Their website says: "When most people think of prayer, they think of asking God for something. Not so in Unity. Unity uses 'affirmative prayer.' Rather than begging or beseeching God, this method involves *connecting with the spirit of God within* and asserting positive beliefs about the desired outcome."[9]

It's possible not everyone in the group has the same beliefs, but essentially Unity doesn't believe in miracles, doesn't believe in a personal God outside of us who intervenes in people's lives, and doesn't believe it's even appropriate to ask for supernatural help.

"So why do we see different results in STEP?" Brown asked. "Look who's doing the praying and how they're doing it."

I thought for a few moments. "This means you can't draw any conclusions about the effectiveness of traditional Christian prayer from STEP," I said.

"That's right," she replied. "None."

With Dr. Shermer's comments in the back of my mind, I asked, "Would you consider STEP to be definitive or a final word on prayer research?"

No hesitation from Dr. Brown. "Not at all," she said.

I posed one more question along those lines: "In the end, does this study tell us *anything* that's helpful?"

She thought for a few moments. "Well," she said, "it is instructive on how *not* to conduct a study of Christian prayer."

A Better Study

In addition to her specific critiques of STEP, Dr. Brown raised several concerns about the overall approach in these "double-blind" prayer studies.

- First, these studies don't take into consideration that healing seems to be clustered in certain geographical areas.
- Second, these studies don't recognize that certain people seem to have a special "anointing" or success rate with healing prayer.
- Third, the people receiving prayer in these studies can't respond with faith, because they don't even know someone is praying for them.

So, Dr. Brown conducted a study that takes these factors into consideration.

And the results were fascinating.

Miracles in Mozambique?

To go to a place that's reporting clusters of healing, Dr. Brown and her team flew to Mozambique, in Africa. Mozambique fits the four characteristics author Tim Stafford (who's written on miracles) says are often shared by places where there are outbreaks of the supernatural:

1. There's illiteracy. Miracles show God's power without language.
2. People don't have a concept of sin and salvation. Stafford wrote, "Miracles demand attention even if you don't yet grasp the nature of your problem and God's redemption."
3. There's limited medical care, making miracles the only hope for the afflicted.
4. The spirit world is very real to people, and "a conflict of spiritual powers is out in the open." Miracles are demonstrations of God's power.[10]

To connect with a ministry that reports a high success rate with healing, Brown's team worked with Heidi and Rolland Baker, missionaries serving in Mozambique for more than twenty years. They have described how healing miracles have accompanied the spread of the gospel there.

Dr. Brown focused on the healing of the blind and deaf (or those with severe vision or hearing problems), because vision and hearing can be scientifically tested. Her team used standard tests and technical equipment to determine the person's level of hearing or vision immediately before prayer. After the prayers were concluded, the patient was promptly tested again.

There was a woman who couldn't see a hand in front of her face at a foot away. Heidi Baker put her arms around this woman, smiled at her, hugged her, then she cried, and prayed for one minute—afterward, the woman was able to read.

In all there were twenty-four subjects who received prayer. The results? "We saw improvement in almost every single subject tested," Brown said. "Some of the results were quite dramatic."

Dr. Brown then mentioned the story of Martine, an elderly blind and deaf woman. Before prayer, Martine had no response at 100 decibels in either ear. That means she couldn't hear a jackhammer if it were being used next to her. After prayer, she responded at 75 decibels in her right ear and 40 decibels in her left ear, which means she could make out conversations.

After a second prayer, Martine's eyesight improved from 20/400 to 20/80 on the vision chart. This would mean she was initially legally blind, but after prayer, she was able to see objects from twenty feet away in the same way a person with normal vision can see that object from eighty feet away.

Dr. Brown's methods were very simple. The only thing that changed between the pre-prayer and post-prayer tests was the fact that someone prayed to Jesus for the person to get better. And virtually everyone did improve to one degree or the other, often astoundingly so.

I asked Dr. Brown whether the study was scientifically sound, and she listed the requirements they met:

- It was published in a peer-reviewed medical journal—meaning doctors from outside the study were able to examine the methods and results.
- They had the proper equipment.
- They used a trained research team.
- They got statistically significant results.
- The study was evaluated and declared scientifically sound by the journal that published it.

"However," I pointed out, "the number of tested people was pretty small."

"There's a misconception that if you've got a small sample, it's not statistically significant. Actually, that's not true," she replied. "With a smaller sample, the effects have to be larger and more consistent in order to achieve statistical significance. And our effects were."

Dr. Brown and her team then did a study in Brazil to check if they would get similar results—and they did. Again, sight and hearing were improved after hands-on prayer was offered in Jesus' name.

In Sao Paulo, for example, a forty-eight-year-old woman named Julia could not see details on faces or read without glasses. "After prayer, she could do both," Dr. Brown said. And "A thirty-eight-year-old woman in Uberlandia could not count fingers from nine feet away. When she opened her eyes after prayer, she could read the name tag of the person who had been praying for her."

Now Dr. Brown's husband, Joshua, is spearheading the Global Medical Research Institute to apply strict scientific methods to investigate claims of miraculous healings.

In the meantime, Candy Gunther Brown's work and analysis has already undermined Dr. Shermer's claim that when research is conducted scientifically, it shows "zero" evidence for the miraculous.

Quite the opposite appears to be true. It seems that, upon further study, the evidence *is* good for the Christian side.

CHAPTER 2

———•———

MEDICAL "MIRACLES"?

When I started writing this book, I knew there was one person I really had to talk to: Dr. Michael Keener. Dr. Keener is the author of a book titled *Miracles: The Credibility of the New Testament Accounts*. To say that the book covers the topic thoroughly would be an understatement; the book is 1,248 pages long!

As Dr. Keener was doing research for his book, the more he discovered, the more convinced he became of two things: 1) that miracles are more common than a lot of people think, and 2) that they are better documented than many skeptics claim. He wrestled with the arguments against miracles by David Hume; he traveled to Africa to investigate claims of miraculous healings; he sifted Scripture; he unearthed examples of modern wonders, marvels, visions, and dreams.

"Everywhere I looked," Keener told me, "I came across events that better fit a supernatural explanation than a naturalistic conclusion."

I asked, "What was the turning point for you?"

His answer turned out to be a very personal one indeed.

The Healing of Thérèse

For years, Dr. Keener had heard vague stories about his wife's older sister, Thérèse Magnouha, who had been— what? Revived? Resuscitated? Raised from the dead? It wasn't until Dr. Keener flew to Africa and trekked through Congo-Brazzaville, where his wife and Thérèse grew up, that he found out firsthand from eyewitnesses what had actually happened. It was the family connection that made this experience especially meaningful for him.

One day when Thérèse was two, her mother went out for a short time to take some food to a neighbor. Keener told me, "When she returned, Thérèse was crying—she had been bitten by a snake. Her mother strapped the child to her back so she could run for help, but she quickly discovered that the child had stopped breathing."

There were no clinics or doctors. Thérèse's mother carried her child up a mountain and back down the other side in order to find a family friend. She calculated that Thérèse had stopped breathing for more than three hours.

Brain damage begins after just six minutes without oxygen.

"With no medical help available, all they could do was to pray to Jesus," Dr. Keener continued. "They did— and as they began to pray, Thérèse began breathing again. She promptly recovered, and by the next day she was fine. She recently completed a graduate-level seminary degree, so there was no brain damage or other problems."

My skepticism kicked in at this point. "With no doctors around, was there any way of knowing whether or not she had actually died?" I asked.

"This is a culture where people personally encounter death a lot more than Westerners do," Keener answered. "They know what death looks like. Plus, a mother has every reason to grasp at the hope of any breath she could find. But let's say she wasn't clinically dead. Nevertheless, at the very minimum, it would be an astounding recovery, especially given the timing—right after the prayers began."

Because of the family connection, the incident resonated deeply with Keener. But it's only one of many miracles described in his book.

A Deaf Child Hears

Dr. Keener told me about the case of a nine-year-old British girl who was diagnosed with deafness in September 1982, probably because of a virus that severely damaged nerves in both of her ears.

"Her case is reported by a well-credentialed physician," Keener said. "What makes this case especially interesting is that there is medical confirmation before the healing and immediately afterward, which is unusual to have."

The child's medical record says she was diagnosed with untreatable deafness in both ears. A doctor told her parents that there was no cure and nothing he could do to repair her damaged nerves. She was outfitted with hearing aids that did help her hear to some degree.

The girl didn't want to wear hearing aids the rest of her life, so she started to pray that God would heal her. Her family and friends joined her. In fact, her mother said she felt a definite prompting to call out for God's help.

"I kept feeling God was telling me to pray specifically for healing," she said. "Passages kept coming out at me as I read: *If you have faith like children . . . If one among you is ill, lay hands . . . Ask and you shall receive . . . Your faith has made you whole.*"

On March 8, 1983, the girl went to the audiologist because one of her hearing aids had been damaged at school. After the doctor examined her ears and refitted her hearing aids, she was sent home.

The next evening, the child suddenly jumped out of her bed without her hearing aids and came bounding down the stairs. "Mummy, I can hear!" she exclaimed.

Her mother, astonished, tested to see if she could detect noises and words—and she could, even whispers. Her mother called the audiologist, who said, "I don't believe you. It is not possible. All right, if some miracle has happened, I am delighted. Have audiograms done."

The following day, the girl was tested, and her audiogram and tympanogram came back fully normal. "I can give no explanation for this," said the audiologist. "I have never seen anything like it in my life."

The girl's doctor ruled out possible medical explanations. In the medical report, the child's ENT (ear, nose, and throat) surgeon used the word "inexplicable" to describe what happened. He wrote, "An audiogram did show her hearing in both ears to be totally and completely normal. I was completely unable to explain this phenomenon but naturally, like her parents, I was absolutely delighted . . . I can think of no rational explanation as to why her hearing returned to normal."[11]

Barbara's Story

Dr. Keener went on to discuss another well-documented case. "I've personally interviewed Barbara, who was diagnosed at the Mayo Clinic with progressive multiple sclerosis," Keener said. "I've confirmed the facts with two physicians who treated her. There are numerous independent witnesses to her condition years of medical records. In fact, two of her doctors were so astounded by her case that they have written about it in books."

When Barbara was in high school, she was a gymnast, and she played flute in the orchestra. But symptoms began appearing: she would trip, she bumped into walls, and was unable to grasp the rings in gym.

Eventually, after her condition got worse, she had spinal taps and other tests, all of which confirmed the diagnosis of progressive multiple sclerosis. After thoroughly examining her case, doctors at the Mayo Clinic agreed with the diagnosis.

Over the next sixteen years, Barbara got worse and worse. She spent months in hospitals, often for pneumonia. One lung functioned at less than fifty percent; the other lung didn't work at all. She needed a tracheotomy tube in order to breathe.

She lost control of her urination and bowels. She went legally blind; she could no longer read, and could see objects only as gray shadows. A feeding tube was inserted into her stomach. "Her abdomen was swollen grotesquely because the muscles of her intestine did not work," one of her doctors said.

Eventually, Barbara needed continuous oxygen, and her muscles and joints were becoming contracted and deformed because she could not use them. "Mayo [Clinic] was her last hope, but they had no recommendations to help stop this progressive wasting disease except to pray for a miracle," another of her doctors said.

By 1981, Barbara had not been able to walk for seven years. She was confined to bed, her body twisted like a pretzel into a fetal position. Her hands were permanently flexed to the point that her fingers nearly touched her wrists. Her feet were locked in a downward position.

One of Barbara's doctor explained to her family that it was just a matter of time before she would die. They agreed not to do any heroics, including CPR or further hospitalization, to keep her alive; this would only prolong the inevitable. Barbara's life expectancy was less than six months.

———————

One day someone called in Barbara's story to the radio station of the Moody Bible Institute in Chicago. The radio station asked listeners to pray fervently for Barbara. Some four hundred and fifty Christians wrote letters to her church saying they were lifting up Barbara in prayer.

On Pentecost Sunday, 1981, her aunt came over to read her some of the letters in which people offered prayers for her healing. Two of Barbara's girlfriends joined them. Suddenly, during a lull in the conversation, Barbara heard a man's voice speak from behind her—even though there was no one else in the room.

The voice had great authority, but also great compassion. The words were clear: "My child, get up and walk!"

When one of Barbara's friends saw that Barbara was getting worked up, she plugged Barbara's tracheotomy hole so Barbara could speak.

"I don't know what you're going to think about this," Barbara said, "but God just told me to get up and walk. I know he really did! Run and get my family. I want them here with us!"

Her friends ran out and yelled for her family, "Come quick; come quick!"

Barbara literally jumped out of bed. She was standing for the first time in years. She took off her oxygen tube. Her vision was back, and she no longer had trouble breathing, even without her oxygen. Her body was no longer twisted, and she could freely move her feet and hands.

Her mother ran into the room and dropped to her knees, feeling Barbara's calves. "You have muscles again!" she exclaimed. Her father came in, hugged her, "and whisked her off for a waltz around the family room," the doctor said.

Everyone moved to the living room to offer a tearful prayer of thanksgiving—although Barbara found it hard to sit still. That evening, there was a worship service at Wheaton Wesleyan Church, where Barbara's family attended. Most of the congregation knew about Barbara's grave condition.

During the service, when the pastor asked if anyone had any announcements, Barbara stepped into the center aisle and casually strolled toward the front, her heart pounding.

Whispers came from all parts of the church. The doctor noted, "People started clapping, and then, as if led by a divine conductor, the entire congregation began to sing: 'Amazing grace, how sweet the sound that saved a wretch like me! I once was lost but now I'm found, was blind but now I see!'"

The next day, Barbara went to her doctor's office for an examination. Seeing her in the hallway, walking toward him, "I thought I was seeing an apparition!" he recalled. "No one had ever seen anything like this before."

He told Barbara, "This is medically impossible. But you are now free to go out and live your life."

A chest X-ray that afternoon showed her lungs were already perfectly normal, with the collapsed lung completely expanded. The tubes in her trachea and abdomen were taken out and she was able to breathe, eat, and do everything else a healthy person can do.

Barbara has now lived for thirty-five years with

no recurrence of her illness. Her doctors marvel at her extraordinary recovery. "I have never witnessed anything like this before or since and considered it a rare privilege to observe the hand of God performing a true miracle," one of them wrote.

Another said, "Both Barbara and I knew who healed her."

I sat in silence for a while, flabbergasted by Barbara's story. Dr. Keener shared my amazement. "When I interviewed Barbara about her case, she was still brimming with excitement, even after all these years," he said.

My mind searched for scientific explanations. Could her recovery be written off as some sort of natural remission? If so, why would it suddenly occur after so many years, right when hundreds of people were praying for her? Remissions typically take place over time, not suddenly and all at once.

Besides, what about the mysterious voice telling her to get up and walk? Or the immediate muscle tone in her atrophied legs? Or the instant and simultaneous healing of her eyesight, lungs, and so on? With so many witnesses of unquestioned integrity and expertise, plus an immense amount of documentation, it was clear that this wasn't a case of misdiagnosis, or fraud, or coincidence, or medical mistakes.

This did seem to be a clear and believable example of a miracle. And Dr. Keener was far from finished. He began to rattle off a series of other amazing stories that he had documented in his book.

Brad's Story

Dr. Keener told me about a neuropsychologist named Ed Wilkinson. Ed's training told him that sick people often use faith as a crutch. They count on God to cure them so they don't have to deal with reality.

Then Ed's eight-year-old son, Brad, was diagnosed with two holes in his heart. Brad's lungs were also damaged. Surgery was scheduled. As the surgery got closer, Brad started giving away his toys—he didn't think he would survive the operation. One day he asked his dad, "Am I going to die?"

That had to be a hard question for a father to answer! After thinking for a moment, Ed told his son that not everyone who has heart surgery dies, but it can happen. Then Brad asked, "Can Jesus heal me?"

Remember, Ed had been taught that trusting God to heal someone was just a way of avoiding reality. But this was his son asking. So he said, "I'll get back to you on that."

Ed spent a few days praying, and he read Philippians 4:13, which says, "I can do all things because Christ gives me strength." Then Ed told his son that God does heal, but even if he didn't heal Brad, they still had hope of eternal life in Jesus.

After that, a visiting pastor asked Brad, "Do you believe that Jesus can heal you?" Brad said yes, and the minister prayed for him.

But hospital tests before Brad's surgery showed that Brad hadn't been healed. He still needed surgery. The next morning, Brad went in for his operation. Surgery was expected to last four hours. But after an hour, the surgeon found Ed in the waiting room and showed him two X-rays.

The first X-ray had been taken the day before. It showed blood leaking from one heart chamber to another. The second X-ray was taken just as surgery started. It showed a wall of some sort where the leak had been. The surgeon said there was nothing wrong with Brad's heart, even though the holes were there the day before. Brad's lungs were also now normal.

"I have not seen this very often," the surgeon said. He explained that every once in a while, a hole in a baby's heart will close up on its own. But it was not supposed to happen in an eight-year-old. "You can count this as a miracle," he said.

The hospital risk manager said firmly, "You can see from the [X-rays]: this was *not* a misdiagnosis." The lung specialist added, "Somebody somewhere must have been praying."

Later, an insurance agent called Ed to complain about the forms he had submitted. "What's a 'spontaneous closure'?" the agent asked.

Ed answered, "A miracle."

Today, Brad is in his thirties with a business and children of his own. He has never had any heart problems since his healing.

The List Goes On

I knew Dr. Keener could go on for hours talking about the cases he had investigated. For example, he has 350 reports just of people who have been healed of blindness. Here are a few cases taken at random from his book:

- A welder named David Dominong suffered third- and fourth-degree burns when he was electrocuted in October 2002. He was hospitalized for more than five weeks and told it could be five years until he would be able to walk again. He was confined to a wheelchair and considering amputation when he received prayer and was at once able to walk and run without help.

- Kuldeep Singh had such bad epilepsy that he would pass out during frequent seizures. Fifteen years ago, Pastor Jarnail Singh prayed that God would heal Kuldeep. Since then, Kuldeep hasn't had a single seizure or needed any treatment.

- Matthew Dawson was hospitalized in Australia with confirmed meningitis in April 2007. He was told he would have to remain under hospital care for weeks or months. But he was healed at the exact moment his father, on another continent, offered prayers for him.

- Mirtha Venero Boza, a medical doctor in Cuba, reports that her baby granddaughter's hand was severely burned by a hot iron. The hand swelled up and skin peeled off. Less than half an hour after prayer, however, the baby's hand was completely healed without medical treatment, as if it had never been burned.

- Dr. John White reports that a woman with tuberculosis of the spine had been unable to walk, but she was instantaneously healed after prayer. Her doctor was amazed to find no evidence of disease in her body. Not only was White the doctor who prayed for her, he later married her.

These are only a few of the hundreds of miracles that Dr. Keener investigated. Although the number of witnesses and the amount of documentation varies in the different cases, many of them seem to provide evidence that even doubters can't argue with.

Why Don't More Miracles Happen Here?

Many of the miracles that Dr. Keener documents in his book happened in North America. But it seems that even more happen in Africa, Asia, and other faraway places. Why would that be?

There seem to be at least two possible reasons for this.

- Keener notes, "In America, we have a lot of advanced medical technology, which is God's gift to us, and we should use it. That's the way he typically brings healing. But in many other places around the world, that's not available, and perhaps God's intervention is the only hope in a lot of instances."
- Miracles seem to happen in places where many people are hearing about God (the God of the Bible—Father, Son, and Holy Spirit) in new ways. It seems that God uses miracles to show his love and power. This is happening in China, the

Philippines, India, Ethiopia, Brazil, and many other countries.

The Miracle Business

As Dr. Keener puts it, "It looks like God is still in the miracle business!"

"And you believe he is?" I asked.

Keener's voice was unwavering. This time he answered not merely as a scholar, but also as a relative of the healed Thérèse.

"Yes, I believe he is."

CHAPTER 3

•——————•

DREAMS AND VISIONS

The brick wall was faded and uneven. The wooden door was more than seven feet tall but less than three feet wide, arched at its top and set in a doorway that was a few feet deep.

Nabeel stood outside in the darkness, peering into the warm glow of an enormous room filled with tables overflowing with mouth-watering food. The people inside were ready to enjoy their feast, but they were all waiting and looking to their left, as if they expected someone to speak before the meal.

Nabeel saw his friend David sitting at a table not far from the doorway. Surprised, he called to get David's attention. "I thought we were going to eat together," Nabeel called out.

David answered, "You never responded."

As he described the scene to me, my friend Nabeel was staring off to the side, his eyes narrowed as if he were reliving the experience. He turned to face me. "That was the whole dream," he said.

"And this came after you had asked God for a clear vision?" I asked.

"That's right," he replied. "I called David the next day and asked him what he thought of my dream."

"David was your Christian friend?"

"My *only* Christian friend. I was a devout Muslim; I didn't like to associate with too many Christians."

"And what did he tell you?"

"He said there was no need to interpret what I had experienced. All I needed to do was open the Bible to Luke 13:22–29."

Then Jesus went through the towns and villages, teaching as he made his way to Jerusalem. Someone asked him, "Lord, are only a few people going to be saved?"

He said to them, "Make every effort to enter through the narrow door, because many, I tell you, will try to enter and will not be able to. Once the owner of the house gets up and closes the door, you will stand outside knocking and pleading, 'Sir, open the door for us.'

"But he will answer, 'I don't know you or where you came from …'

"There will be weeping there, and gnashing of teeth, when you see Abraham, Isaac and Jacob and all the prophets in the kingdom of God, but you yourselves thrown out. People will come from east and west and north and south, and will take their places at the feast in the kingdom of God."

"I was standing at the door and it had not yet closed, but it was clear I would not be at this banquet of God—*this heaven*—unless I responded to the invitation," Nabeel said. "The door would be shut for good; the feast would go on without me, forever."

"How did that make you feel?"

He paused before answering. "Chilled. Frightened. Alone. *Desperate*."

"That passage in Luke—how many times had you read it before that night?" I asked.

Nabeel looked surprised by my question. "Not once," he said. "I had never read *any* of the New Testament before—and yet I saw that passage played out in my dream."

"How do you account for that?" I asked.

"I'm a man of science. A medical doctor. I deal with flesh and bones, with evidence and facts and logic. But *this*," Nabeel said, searching for the right words, "this was the exact vision I needed. It was a miracle. A miracle that opened the door for me."

Awakening the Muslim World

This dream was key in leading my friend Nabeel Qureshi to faith in Jesus. He is just one of numerous Muslims who have had visions or dreams that have brought them out of Islam and into Christianity.

In fact, more Muslims have become Christians in the last couple of decades than in the previous fourteen hundred years since Muhammad, and it's estimated that a quarter to a third of them had a dream or vision of Jesus that pointed them to faith in him. If those statistics are accurate, then this phenomenon of Jesus supernaturally appearing to people is one of the most significant spiritual awakenings in the world today.

I talked with Ravi Zacharias, a speaker and Christian apologist who goes to many Islamic countries, where it's tough to talk about Jesus. He told me that nearly every Muslim who has come to follow Christ has done so for one of two reasons. First, because of a Christian who showed them the love of Christ. Or second, because of a vision, dream, or some other supernatural intervention.

Angels and visions are very important in Islam. Ravi believes that God uses that sensitivity to the supernatural world when he speaks in visions and dreams and reveals himself to Muslims.

In the Bible, God often used dreams and visions to

further his plans. From Abraham, Joseph, and Samuel in the Old Testament to Zacharias, John, and Cornelius in the New Testament, there are about two hundred biblical examples.

Today, reports of dreams and visions seem to cluster among believers of Islam, from Indonesia to Pakistan to the Gaza Strip.

Why is this happening now? Why among Muslims? What does Jesus tell these individuals that so radically rocks their world? And if Jesus can appear in dreams and visions like this, why doesn't he show himself that way to everyone?

To get some answers, I went to talk with Pastor Tom Doyle, an author and missionary to the Middle East who is an expert on dreams and visions experienced by Muslims.

The Man in the White Robe

Pastor Doyle and his wife, JoAnn, were in Gaza City in Palestine shortly after the terrorist attacks of 9/11. A woman in a hijab (headscarf) came running up, grabbed Doyle's arm, and said, "You're from America, aren't you?"

When he admitted that he was, the woman asked, "When the buildings came down on 9/11, did you see the video of people in Gaza cheering and celebrating?"

Doyle told her that he had seen it on TV.

The woman said, "Not me. I was crying for those people. They didn't deserve to die. That was wrong. I'm very sorry." She tapped her heart before walking away.

"That was the day that God started to create space in my heart for Muslims," Pastor Doyle told me. "It comes down to this: Are we able to see through Jesus' eyes and not our own? He filters out all the news and prejudice. Once you have his eyes, you see people for who they are—made in his image."

Then Doyle told me about the first time he visited Jerusalem and met with a group of Muslims who had become Christians.

"One of them, Rami, said he had been a fervent Muslim when he started to have dreams about Jesus. He said they were different than anything he had ever experienced. Often dreams are fuzzy or confused, but these were bright and laser focused—and they kept coming."

He saw Jesus in a white robe, and Jesus told Rami that he loved him. They were at a lake, and Rami said he saw himself going to Jesus and hugging him.

Pastor Doyle said, "I didn't know if Rami was nuts or what. But over and over, from a variety of people, I started hearing the same basic story: Jesus in a white robe, saying he loves them, saying he died for them, telling them to follow him. It started to snowball—in Iran, Iraq, Syria, all over. There were even ads placed in Egyptian newspapers."

The ads said, "Have you seen the man in a white robe in your dreams? He has a message for you. Call this number." Because so many Muslims were having these dreams, Christian ministries had placed these ads in an attempt to reach them.

"You're the One! You're the One!"

I asked Doyle if he would give me a typical example of how these dreams play out in someone's life. He chose the story of what happened to Kamal, a Christian and underground church planter in Egypt, and a Muslim mother we'll call Noor. (Pastor Doyle changes names of the people he talks about in the Middle East to protect their identity and keep them from potential danger. The names in these stories have all been changed.)

Kamal was busy with his work one day, but he felt God was leading him to go to the Khan el-Khalili Friday Market in Cairo. Honestly, it was the last place he wanted to go. It was right before Muslim prayers, and the market was crowded and noisy. But he went because he felt 100 percent convinced that God had a special assignment for him.

A Muslim woman named Noor, covered head to toe in traditional clothing, spotted him from a distance and started yelling, "You're the one! You're the one!" She pushed through the crowd and made a beeline for him. She said, "You were in my dream last night! Those clothes—you were wearing those clothes. For sure, it was you."

Kamal quickly sensed what was motivating her. "Was I with Jesus?" he asked.

"Yes," she replied. "Jesus was with us."

Later she explained: "Jesus walked with me alongside a lake and he told me how much he loves me. His love was different from anything I've ever experienced. I've never felt so much peace. I didn't want him to leave. I asked this Jesus, 'Why are you visiting me, a poor Muslim mother with eight children?' And all he said was, 'I love you, Noor. I have given everything for you. I died for you.'"

She said that as Jesus turned to leave, he told her, "Ask my friend tomorrow about me. He will tell you all you need in order to understand why I've visited you."

She replied to Jesus, "But who is your friend?"

Jesus said, "Here is my friend," and he pointed to a person who was behind him in the dream. "He has been walking with us the whole time we've been together."

There in the marketplace, Noor said to Kamal, "Even though you had walked with us around the lake, I hadn't seen anyone but Jesus. I thought I was alone with him. His face was magnificent. I couldn't take my eyes off him. Jesus did not tell me your name, but you were wearing the same clothes you have on right now, and your glasses—they're the same too. I knew I would not forget your smile."

Soon Kamal and Noor were in a deep discussion about faith that lasted some three hours. "I have never been loved like I was when Jesus walked with me in that dream," Noor told him. "I felt no fear. For the first time in my life, I felt no shame. Even though he's a man, I wasn't intimidated. I didn't feel threatened. I felt . . . perfect peace."

Kamal explained to her that only Jesus can bring her that kind of peace. "That's what Jesus wants to give you," Kamal told her. "Before he went to the cross, Jesus said, 'Peace I leave with you; my peace I give you.' You will not—cannot—find peace like that with anyone else. No one but Jesus even has it to offer."

I was mesmerized by Noor's story. "Did she come to faith in Christ?" I asked Pastor Doyle.

"Not on that day," he answered. "She's counting the cost, even as Jesus himself said we should. And the cost to her in Egypt could be very steep. She said she wants to find out all she can about Jesus. There are a lot of people praying for her."

From Terrorist to Church Planter

Pastor Doyle went on to tell me about Omar, a Palestinian man he recently met in Jerusalem. Omar grew up in a refugee camp. He hated Israel. He told Pastor Doyle that his goal in life was to kill as many Jews as he could.

One day, Omar was on his way to meet with people who work with the terrorist organization Hamas. He didn't know anything about Jesus, but all of a sudden, a man in a white robe was standing in front of him in the street and pointing at him. The man said, "Omar, this is not the life I have planned for you. You turn around. Go home. I have another plan for you."

Something about the man impressed Omar so much that he turned around and went home. Later that same day, someone was moving into an apartment across the hall from him. He found out the new tenant was a Christian. Omar told him about the experience he had and asked, "What does it mean?" This Christian spent time with him, took him through the Scriptures, and led him to Jesus. Today, Omar is an underground church planter.

Another man we'll call Osama was part of the Palestinian Authority. He started having dreams about Jesus. Pastor Doyle says, "He went to his imam (the prayer leader of his mosque), who told him to read the Qur'an more. But the more he read the Qur'an, the more he had Jesus dreams. The imam told him to get more involved in the mosque, so he did—still, more Jesus dreams. The imam said to make the Hajj (a holy pilgrimage) to the city of Mecca."

I could picture this person among the throngs at Mecca, walking around the Kaaba, a black building in the center of the most sacred mosque in Islam—and a building often referred to as "the house of Allah." One of the five pillars of Islam says that if a Muslim is able, he should make the Hajj pilgrimage once in his lifetime and walk seven times around the Kaaba. More than a million people walk counterclockwise around the Kaaba during this five-day period.

The people are supposed to look at the Kaaba and say their prayers. But when Osama looked, on top of the Kaaba he saw the Jesus from his dreams. Jesus looked directly at him and said, "Osama, leave this place. You're going in the wrong direction. Leave and go home." So he did.

Later, a Christian shared the gospel with Osama, and he put his faith in Christ. Today, Pastor Doyle told me, this man has such love for Jesus that you can literally see it on his face.

Jesus and Islam

One fact seemed clear: most of the people having these dreams were not naturally inclined to imagine a vision of the Jesus of Christianity. Many live in countries where they never see pictures of Jesus or hear about the Jesus of the Bible.

When Jesus tells them he died for them, that's different from everything they've learned. Islam teaches that

Jesus was a prophet, but, as Pastor Doyle puts it, "The Qur'an says Jesus didn't die on the cross, that Allah does not have a son, and that nobody can pay for the sins of another. The very things that Christianity says are essential to faith are explicitly denied in Islamic teachings."

Pastor Doyle goes on to say that when he tries to talk about the Christian faith with Muslims, they have three common objections. They may believe that the Bible has been corrupted and can't be true. They may think that Christians worship three gods, because Christians talk about the Father, Son, and Holy Spirit. Or they may point to the way Christians slaughtered Muslims during the Crusades.

"These are some of the big boulders on the path between them and the real Jesus," Doyle told me. "But in these high-definition Jesus dreams, they're gently walked around those boulders. They see Jesus for who he is, and now they're motivated to learn more.

"It's interesting," he continued, "that after having a dream or vision, the typical objections that Muslims raise against Christianity disappear. I've never met someone who had a Jesus dream who is still hung up on the deity of Christ (whether Jesus is God or not) or the veracity of the Scriptures (whether the Bible is true or not). Instantly, they know this: Jesus is more than just a prophet. And they want to know more about him."

I noticed that in Doyle's description of these dreams,

he doesn't say the Muslim immediately puts his or her trust in Jesus. I said to him, "It seems that people don't go to sleep Muslims, have a Jesus dream, and then wake up as Christians."

"That's right. I've never heard of that happening," Doyle replied. "Usually, the dream points them toward someone who can teach them from the Bible and present the gospel, like Noor in the Cairo marketplace. Or like Omar, who was steered away from meeting with Hamas, went home, and 'coincidentally' found a Christian moving in across the hall. The dreams motivate them to seek the real Jesus and to find the truth in Scripture."

Why Not Here?

I still wondered why God was working so powerfully in this way in the Middle East, but not so much in North America. Pastor Doyle had some ideas.

"The Western world doesn't need dreams and visions— we have easy access to God's Word. But it's estimated that 50 percent of Muslims around the world can't read, so how are we going to get the Scriptures to them? And 86 percent of Muslims don't know a Christian, so who's going to share the gospel with them? In light of these realities, how might God reach them? I believe God is fair—the Bible says, 'Will not the Judge of all the earth do right?'[12] I think he's going to find a way to bring Jesus to them.

"Put yourself in God's position," he said, pointing toward me. "You want your message to get around the world. Huge numbers of Muslims—people you love deeply—don't have access to Christians or the Bible. Now, what's your plan B? How would you get their attention—especially in a culture that values dreams? It's just like our loving God to do something radical to reach them. Extreme times require extreme measures."

As I chatted with Doyle, I had to confess that I felt a little jealous of people who have had Jesus dreams. I've followed Christ for several decades now. I've studied the Bible. I've felt God's presence, guidance, and power in my life. But to have a vivid and vibrant dream of talking with a white-robed Jesus and hearing his voice offer love, grace, and acceptance—well, I have to admit that would be awesome.

"Do you envy them?" I said to Doyle as we were wrapping up our conversation. "Do you wish Jesus would appear to you in a dream?"

"Wow," he said, just thinking about the prospect. "Who wouldn't want an encounter like that? Yeah, it would be incredible. But I've got the Scriptures to tell me about Jesus; I have his Spirit to affirm and guide me; and I know I'll see him face-to-face someday."

His face looked content. "Yes," he said finally, "that's enough for me."

A Kitchen, a Sandwich, an Angel, a Prophecy

Jesus has never appeared to me in a dream. But I actually did have a dream in which I spoke with an angel—and received a prophecy that came true sixteen years later. It was the most dramatic—and puzzling—dream I had as a kid. I'm still amazed by its clarity and vibrancy, as well as the emotional impact it had on me at the time.

When I was about twelve years old, before I became an atheist, I dreamed I was making a sandwich for myself in the kitchen. Suddenly, an angel suddenly appeared and started telling me about how wonderful and glorious heaven is. I listened for a while, and then said matter-of-factly, "I'm going there"—meaning, of course, at the end of my life.

The angel's reply stunned me. "How do you know?"

How did I know? What kind of question is that? "Well, uh, I've tried to be a good kid," I stammered. "I've tried to do what my parents say. I've tried to behave. I've been to church."

The angel said, "That doesn't matter."

Now I was staggered. How could it not matter? Panic rose in me. I couldn't open my mouth to respond.

The angel let me worry for a few moments. Then he said, "Someday you'll understand." Instantly, he was gone—and I woke up in a sweat. This was the only dream I can recall from my childhood.

Over the years, I came to reject the possibility of the supernatural and even God himself. I was an atheist for a long period of time. But sixteen years after that dream, the angel's prophecy came true.

In a church meeting in a suburban Chicago movie theater, I understood the message of grace for the first time. I realized that I couldn't earn my way to heaven by being good. It was all a free gift from God—a gift that I needed to receive in repentance and faith.

The moment this clicked for me, a vivid memory came into my mind: the angel who had foretold that someday I would understand the gospel. Ultimately, it was this good news that went on to change my life and eternity.

Was my dream a supernatural intervention? Would it qualify as a miracle? I'll leave it to you to make your own judgment. But in a small way, I can relate to some of these stories of dreams and visions coming from the Middle East.

PART 2

The Most
SPECTACULAR
MIRACLES

CHAPTER 4

—•————•—

THE ASTONISHING
MIRACLE OF CREATION

When William Lane Craig was a teenager, he doubted that Jesus' mother, Mary, could have been a virgin. Why? Because a Y chromosome would have had to be created out of nothing in Mary's ovum, since she didn't possess the genetic material to produce a male child.

"But then," he said, "it occurred to me that if I really do believe in a God who created the universe, then for him to create a Y chromosome would be no problem!"

In short, if God created the laws of nature when he spoke the universe into being, then it would be easy for him to occasionally intervene in order to do miracles of all sorts, from the truly astounding (like raising someone from the dead) to the more subtle (like supernaturally encouraging someone who is struggling).

Without a doubt, the granddaddy of all miracles is

the creation of the universe from nothing. If Genesis 1:1 is correct when it says, "In the beginning God created the heavens and the earth," then it's not hard to believe that God can do other miracles too. If God can command an entire universe and even time itself to leap into existence, then walking on water would be like a stroll in the park, and a resurrection would be as simple as a snap of the fingers.

Of course, people try to come up with other explanations for the origin and fine-tuning of the universe. Maybe the universe didn't have a cause. Perhaps there was never an absolute beginning for everything. Or there could even be a multitude of universes, each one with randomly selected laws and physics, and ours just happened to be habitable.

Can we ever know for sure whether the universe is a cosmic accident or a miracle? Or should we shrug our shoulders and say that we don't know where everything came from?

To find answers to questions like these, I went to talk to a physicist named Michael Strauss.

Dr. Strauss first became interested in science as a kid. He lived in Huntsville, Alabama, where NASA built the first stage of the mighty Saturn V rocket that later took astronauts to the moon. There's still enthusiasm in his voice when he says, "They'd light those boosters to test them and—*wow!*—the whole town would shake!"

Now Dr. Strauss is a professor of physics at the

University of Oklahoma, and he researches at the Large Hadron Collider in Switzerland, smashing protons together in order to understand, among other things, fundamental particles called top quarks. In fact, he was on the team whose discoveries helped find the famous Higgs boson known as the "God particle" in 2012 (which was named that because it was so essential and difficult to find, not because of any God-like characteristics).

Strauss's studies of the world's tiniest particles have become more and more relevant to our understanding of the beginnings and workings of our world and our vast universe. That's because the collider he works with can simulate what the universe may have been like a trillionth of a second after it first began. So I wanted his scientific opinion about whether anything he's studied points to God as the creator of quarks, Higgs bosons, and other building blocks of nature. Is there any evidence for the miracle of creation?

Seeing God in Everyday Nature

"When I go to the lab, I don't expect to see the supernatural," Dr. Strauss told me. "If miracles happened all the time, we wouldn't be able to study the usual way nature works. But just because something works a certain way most of the time with the laws of nature, doesn't mean there can't be exceptions."

But even without miracles, the science of "the usual way nature works" can point to God, he explained. "The Bible says it's through the natural processes of nature that we most commonly see evidence for God, not just through his miracles. Romans 1:20 tells us that God's invisible qualities are clearly seen—through what? Through what he has made. And Psalm 19:1 says, 'The heavens declare the glory of God; the skies proclaim the work of his hands.' So, frankly, we don't necessarily need miracles to find evidence for God; it's right there, embedded in the natural processes that he has created and that we, as scientists, are studying."

It was a good reminder that when protons collide and explode into even tinier particles, scientists are getting a glimpse into the incredible complexity and wonder of God's creativity, just as we detect his supernatural qualities when we watch an awesome thunderstorm or look at the galaxy of stars winking in the night sky.

The Big Bang

Going back to the ancient Greeks, most scientists believed the universe has always existed—that it didn't have a beginning.

When Albert Einstein came up with his general theory of relativity in 1915 and applied it to the universe as a whole, he was shocked. The theory showed that the universe should either be growing or collapsing. Other scientists, using Einstein's theories, concluded the universe is indeed expanding. In other words, in the past, the universe was smaller than it is now.

Imagine that somehow you could watch a video of the universe expanding—getting bigger and bigger. Mindboggling, isn't it? Now imagine that you could play the video backward. You'd see the universe getting smaller and smaller. If you could go back far enough, you would see it shrink down to its very beginnings.

That's what was so shocking to Albert Einstein and other scientists. They didn't think that the universe *had* a beginning. Now they were seeing evidence that it did.

That beginning, according to scientists, was what we call the big bang.

Christians and the Big Bang Theory

What do Christians think about the big bang theory? (The science one, not the TV show.)

Well, that depends on who you ask.

Some Christians believe that the big bang theory contradicts the Bible. Genesis 1 talks about God creating the world in six days, with human beings being created on the sixth day. The big bang theory implies that the universe came into its current form over a much longer period of time. Humans, according to this theory, came on the scene much later.

Another argument that some Christians make is that the earth cannot possibly be billions of years old, as the big bang theory suggests. They believe that the earth is about 6,000 years old—that it was created around 4000 B.C. These Christians (often called "young-earth creationists") get that date by adding up the ages of people in the genealogy lists in the Bible and counting backward to Adam.[13]

Christians who reject the big bang theory might say that when it's the Bible vs. science, the Bible is right.

Other Christians say that the Bible and what we learn from the natural world simply *won't* be in conflict, because both the Bible and the world come from God. They say that if what science learns from the natural world seems to disagree with what we learn from the Bible, it's because either 1) we haven't understood the science correctly or 2) we haven't understood the Bible correctly.

Because there is so much good scientific evidence for the big bang theory, they say, maybe the problem isn't with the big bang but with how we understand Genesis. They point out that at one time, Galileo's statement that the earth revolves around the sun was considered anti-biblical, but now Christians accept that scientific discovery.

Many Christians believe that the six days of creation described in Genesis 1 are not supposed to be understood as twenty-four-hour days. They point out that the Bible never talks about how old the earth is, and that there could be gaps in the lists of ages that young-earth creationists use to calculate the date of creation.

Other Christians would argue that the point of Genesis 1 and 2 is not to tell us *how* the world was created, but *who* created it.

A lot of people would probably be surprised to learn that one of the scientists who first suggested the big bang theory was a Catholic priest. His name was Georges Lemaître.[14] You might expect that Monseigneur Lemaître would have faced opposition from the Catholic Church, as had Galileo and other scientists before him. But in fact, Pope Pius XII affirmed the big bang theory. He saw it as scientific confirmation of a Creator God. He said:

It would seem that present-day science, with one sweep back across the centuries, has succeeded in bearing witness to the august instant of . . . Let there be Light, when along with matter, there burst forth from nothing a sea of light and radiation, and the elements split and churned and formed into millions of galaxies . . . Science has confirmed . . . the world came forth from the hands of the Creator. Hence, creation took place. We say "Therefore, there is a Creator. Therefore, God exists!"[15]

More recently, Pope Francis also stated that there is no conflict between the Christian faith and the theory. He said, "The big bang, which is today posited as the origin of the world, does not contradict the divine act of creation; rather, it requires it."[16]

This isn't just a Catholic thing, though. Many Protestant churches have also made statements affirming that there is no conflict between Christianity and the big bang theory, and many individual Christians in a wide variety of churches feel the same way.

Scientists and the Big Bang Theory

So how do scientists view the big bang theory?

Interestingly, when the theory was first proposed in the 1920s, some scientists rejected it. Why? Because if the big bang really happened, that meant that the universe *hadn't* always existed. It meant that the universe had a beginning. That went against everything that scientists had previously believed.

In fact, the name "big bang" was originally used by a scientist making fun of the theory. That scientist, Fred Hoyle, thought the idea that the universe had a beginning was ridiculous. And he, like many other scientists at the time, thought the description of the big bang—something created out of nothing—was far too similar to what religious people believed.

Over the years, though, the evidence for the big bang has been growing. Here are three discoveries Dr. Strauss says confirm the big bang theory:

- 1929: "Astronomer Edwin Hubble discovered the so-called 'red shift' in light coming from distant galaxies, which is the result of galaxies literally flying apart from each other at enormous speeds. This showed our universe is rapidly expanding."
- 1964: "Arno Penzias and Robert Wilson measured the cosmic background microwave radiation, which showed that the leftover heat from the big bang was minus 450 degrees Fahrenheit. This is exactly what we would expect if the big bang occurred."
- 1995: The origin of light elements was discovered. Science shows that heavier elements that formed later in stars were thrown into space by supernovae, but lighter elements (such as helium and hydrogen) would have needed to form in a much hotter environment, such as the big bang. "When we measure the amount of these two elements in the universe, we find they are precisely what the theory predicted to within one part in ten thousand."

In addition, recently scientists have found these further evidences that support the big bang theory:

- 1995: Astrophysicist Arthur Davidsen announced the discovery of helium in interplanetary space. The amount of this element in the universe is precisely what the theory predicted to within one part in ten thousand.[17]

- 2017: The Nobel Prize for Physics was awarded to three scientists involved in the discovery of gravitational waves. Gravitational waves are ripples in time and space. They are further evidence of the rapid expansion of the universe at the big bang.[18]

As more and more discoveries are made, the evidence for the big bang is getting stronger. I asked Dr. Strauss for his opinion, as a nuclear physicist and a Christian.

"Given the evidence, in my opinion not believing in the big bang is like believing the Earth is flat," he said. "To me, the data are that strong. The big bang is the origin of everything we know—space, time, matter, and energy."

Another Christian scientist, named William Lane Craig, has popularized the so-called *kalam* argument, which says:

- Whatever begins to exist has a cause.
- The universe began to exist.
- Therefore, the universe has a cause.[19]

He points to God as the one who put it into motion, and the big bang as evidence of a start to creation.

"What do you think of the *kalam* argument?" I asked.

"It's extremely strong," Dr. Strauss answered. "Think about it: Is there anything that comes into existence without a cause behind it? And we know from the evidence that the universe did come into existence. If those two things are true, then the conclusion [inevitably] follows: the universe has a cause."

CHAPTER 5

• — •

OUR MIRACULOUS
UNIVERSE AND PLANET

Imagine that you are in a control room. Everywhere you look, you see hundreds of dials, buttons, and knobs. Each one controls a different variable that makes intelligent life possible. And each one has to be tuned exactly right. According to Dr. Strauss, "If you turn any one of them a little to the left or a little to the right—*poof!* Intelligent life becomes impossible anywhere in the universe."

Over the last fifty years, physicists have discovered that the variables in the universe are just that finely tuned. Variables like the strength of gravity, the distance the earth is from the sun, and many, many more each have to be just right in order for life to exist.

And, obviously, each variable is. The universe has everything we need to live—in other words, the universe is "fine-tuned" for human existence.

And that's not only the opinion of Christian scientists. Virtually every scientist agrees the universe is finely tuned—the question is, how did it get this way?

Matter Matters

I asked physicist Dr. Strauss for a few examples of that fine-tuning.

"One parameter is the amount of matter in the universe. As the universe expands, all matter is attracted to other matter by gravity. If there were too much matter, the universe would collapse on itself before stars and planets could form. If there were too little matter, stars and planets could never coalesce (form)." The particles would just drift off into space.

"How finely tuned is the amount of matter?" I wanted to know.

"It turns out that shortly after the big bang, the amount of matter in the universe was precisely tuned to one part in a trillion trillion trillion trillion trillion," Strauss replied. "That's a ten with sixty zeroes after it! In other words, throw in a dime's worth of extra matter, and the universe wouldn't exist."

Strauss continued. "British physicist Paul Davies—who's an agnostic—said 'such stunning accuracy is surely one of the great mysteries of cosmology.'"[20]

"How does he try to explain it away?"

"He said cosmic inflation might force the universe to have exactly the right amount of matter."

"Does that make sense?"

"Even if you assume cosmic inflation is a mechanism that works, it doesn't make the fine-tuning problem go away."

"Why not?"

"Here's an illustration. If I tried to pour gasoline into my lawn mower through a really small hole, it would be very difficult. Why? Because the hole is finely tuned (is a certain size). But if I take the same fuel and pour it into a funnel, then I can easily fill the gas tank. Now, does the fact that I have a funnel—a mechanism that works—mean I've eliminated the fine-tuning problem? No, of course not. If I have a mechanism that works, it also points to a designer."

In other words, if you explain the fine-tuning of matter by cosmic inflation, you still have a designer who caused the cosmic inflation.

Holding Atoms Together

Then Strauss offered another fine-tuning example from something he studies in his research—the strong nuclear force. "This is what holds together the nucleus of atoms," he explained. "Ultimately, it's the strength of this force that produces the periodic table of elements."

I pictured in my mind the colorful periodic table I studied in chemistry class, which displays all naturally occurring elements from atomic numbers 1 (hydrogen) to 94 (plutonium), as well as several heavier elements that have only been made in laboratories or nuclear reactors.

"What happens if you manipulate the strong nuclear force?" I asked.

"If you were to make it just 2 percent stronger while all the other constants stayed the same, you'd add a lot more elements to the periodic table, but they would be radioactive and life-destroying. Plus, you'd have very little hydrogen in the universe—and no hydrogen, no water, no life."

"What if the force were weaker?"

"Decrease the force by a mere 5 percent, and all you'd have would be hydrogen. Again, a dead universe. Another area of my research involves quarks, which make up neutrons and protons. If we change the light quark mass just 2 or 3 percent, there would be no carbon in the universe."

"And no carbon means—what?" I asked.

Dr. Strauss gestured at the two of us. "That you and I wouldn't be sitting here."

The examples could go on and on. For instance, there are two forces that have to be in a very precise ratio. (They are called electromagnetic force and the gravitational force.) It is fine-tuned to one part in ten thousand trillion trillion trillion. I don't fully understand this ratio, but scientists say that it's important.

Here's an illustration of that same idea that I do understand: Imagine covering a *billion* North American continents with dimes up to the moon—238,000 miles high. Choose one dime at random, paint it red, and put it somewhere in the piles. Blindfold a friend and have him pick out one dime from the billion continents. What are the odds he'd choose the red dime? One in ten thousand trillion trillion trillion.[21]

Fine-tuning like that doesn't just happen by chance.

Our Place in the Universe

Dr. Strauss went on to say, "Not only is our universe precisely tuned to a breathtaking degree, but our planet is also remarkably and fortuitously situated so that life would be possible."

To have a planet like ours where life exists, Strauss says you need several things:

"First, you need to be in the right kind of galaxy. There are three types of galaxies: elliptical, spiral, and irregular. You need to be in a spiral galaxy, like we are, because it's the only kind that produces the right heavy elements and has the right radiation levels.

"But you can't live just anywhere in the galaxy. If you're too close to the sun, there's too much radiation and there's also a black hole, which you want to avoid. If you're too far from the center, you won't have the right heavy elements; you'd lack the oxygen and carbon you'd need. You have to live in the so-called 'Goldilocks Zone,' or the galactic habitable zone, where life could exist." And by "life," Dr. Strauss is referring to anything more complex than bacteria.

"To have life, you need a star like our sun. Our sun is what's called a Class G star that has supported stable planet orbits in the right location for a long time. The star must be in its middle age, so its luminosity is stabilized. It has to be a bachelor star"—which means it's not orbiting another star, as many stars do. "Plus, the star should be a third-generation star, like our sun." Third-generation stars have enough material to create rocky planets (like Earth) and carbon-based life forms (like us).

"You need a moon like ours—it's very rare to have just one large moon—in order to stabilize the Earth's tilt.

"Also, it's nice to have a huge planet like Jupiter nearby to act like a vacuum cleaner by attracting potentially deadly comets and meteors away from you."

And those are just a few of the conditions that have to be just right for our planet to support life. You need the right rotation rate, amount of water, and tilt. The planet needs to be the right size so gravity allows gases such as methane to escape, but also allows the gases we need, like oxygen, to stay.

In fact, there are at least 322 conditions that have to be exactly right for a planet to support life. That means the odds of having any higher life-supporting planet would be one in a million trillion.

Dr. Strauss said, "In science, we have a phrase for probabilities like that."

"Really? What is it?"

He grinned. "Ain't gonna happen."

Design without a Designer?

You don't have to be a Christian to think that all this fine-tuning is not a coincidence.

Here is what Dr. Paul Davies, a professor of physics at Arizona State University and an agnostic, says. "There is, for me, powerful evidence that there is something going on behind it all. It seems as though somebody has fine-tuned nature's numbers to make the universe … The impression of design is overwhelming."[22]

British cosmologist Edward R. Harrison was not a

Christian, but he wrote, "Here is the cosmological proof of the existence of God. The fine-tuning of the universe provides *prima facie* evidence of deistic design."[23]

Even so, some scientists have come up with bizarre explanations for how this fine-tuning could have happened without God.

For instance, John Barrow and Frank Tipler, in their book *The Anthropic Cosmological Principle*, give this argument:

- The universe is clearly designed.
- Design requires intelligence.
- Intelligence is only possessed by humans.

So they hypothesize that humans will continue to evolve until someday they become like gods—*at which point they reach back in time and create the universe themselves!*

Obviously, this theory is not widely accepted.

Neither is the idea that our universe is actually a *Matrix*-like simulation being run on a giant computer by some superprogrammer. After all, that still raises the problem of how the superprogrammer's universe came into existence.

Then there's the idea that black holes lead to the creation of baby universes. These then create more universes through black holes, and so on for eternity. But that leaves open the question of where the first black hole–producing universe came from.

Another hypothesis that quickly evaporated is that the fine-tuning is the result of random chance. The odds of that, scientists say, are functionally equivalent to impossible. "The precision is so utterly fantastic, so mathematically breathtaking, that it's just plain silly to think it could have been an accident," Dr. William Lane Craig said.[24]

Physicist Robin Collins gave me this analogy when I wrote *The Case for a Creator*: Imagine that I bet you I could flip a coin and get heads fifty times in a row. If I really did it, you wouldn't accept the results. You'd know that the odds against me getting that many heads in a row are too high—about one chance in a million billion. The fact that I could do it against such large odds would be strong evidence that the game had been rigged. And the same is true for the fine-tuning of the universe. Before you'd decide that random chance was responsible, you'd decide that there is strong evidence that the universe was rigged. In other words, designed.

Another theory, called the multiverse theory, is that there is a nearly infinite number of other universes. If the dials of physics were twirled at random in all of those, sooner or later one universe would hit the jackpot and get the right conditions for life.

Scientists aren't in agreement about the multiverse theory. Stephen Hawking, a highly respected physicist and cosmologist, has argued in favor of the theory. Others point out that the theory can't be tested and there is no observable evidence. One article in *Astronomy* magazine says the theory "straddles a strange world between science fiction and a plausible hypothesis."[25]

Oxford philosopher Richard Swinburne was blunt about what he thinks. "To postulate a trillion trillion other universes, rather than one God, in order to explain the orderliness of our universe, seems the height of irrationality."[26]

The God Option

The incredible precision of the universe and our planet is not just intriguing. It's compelling evidence for a miracle-working Designer.

Dr. Strauss said, "Let's go back to what I know for a fact as a scientist. I know there's one universe that appears to have a beginning, which is incredibly calibrated in a way that defies naturalistic explanations, and there's a highly improbable planet whose unlikely conditions allow us to exist. To me, all of that begs for a divine explanation."

But here's a question skeptics frequently ask: If this God made the universe, then who made him?

"Nobody," Dr. Strauss quickly said. "The *kalam* argument doesn't say, 'Whatever *exists* has a cause.' It says, 'Whatever *begins* to exist has a cause.' By definition, God never *began* to exist; he has always existed. He is a necessary, self-existent, eternal being. That's part of the definition of God. Why assume a triangle has three sides? Because that's part of what it means to be a triangle."

I also recall what William Lane Craig once told me: "Atheists themselves used to be very comfortable in maintaining that the universe is eternal and uncaused. The problem is that they can no longer hold that position because of modern evidence that the universe started with the big bang. So they can't legitimately object when I make the same claim about God—he is eternal and he is uncaused."[27]

I asked Dr. Strauss, "If God is the most likely explanation for our universe and planet, then what can we logically deduce about him from the scientific evidence?"

He listed several things. In his words:

First, [God] must be transcendent, because he exists apart from his creation.

Second, he must be immaterial or spirit, since he existed before the physical world.

Third, he must be timeless or eternal, since he existed before physical time was created.

Fourth, he must be powerful, given the immense energy of the big bang.

Fifth, he must be smart, given the fact that the big bang was not some chaotic event but was masterfully finely tuned.

Sixth, he must be personal, because a decision had to be made to create.

Seventh, he must be creative—just look at the wonders of the universe.

Eighth, he must be caring, because he so purposefully crafted a habitat for us.

"All the qualities we've [listed] are consistent with the God of the Bible," Dr. Strauss pointed out. "If there's just one creator, then that rules out polytheism. Since he's outside of creation, this rules out pantheism. The universe is not cyclical, which violates the tenets of Eastern religions. And the big bang contradicts ancient religious assumptions that the universe is static."

The purpose of my visit had been fulfilled. Thinking over the case that Dr. Strauss had built, I concluded that the existence of a miracle-working creator—who matches the description of the God of the Bible—had been established beyond a reasonable doubt.

CHAPTER 6

The Miracle

of the

Resurrection

Even for an experienced cold-case homicide investigator, this was a big challenge. Detective J. Warner Wallace had used his extensive skills to solve murders that were decades old. But he had never tackled a case that stretched back for *two thousand* years.

What's more, this time he wasn't merely trying to find the criminal. Instead, he was trying to find out whether the victim was truly dead—and whether he had risen from the dead three days later.

Quite a job for someone who was at the time a hyperskeptical atheist.

Detective Wallace is the son of a cop and the father of a cop. He has worked on a SWAT team, the gang detail, and robbery and murder cases. Then he became a member of a cold-case homicide unit, assigned to crack murders that nobody else had been able to solve.

He was so good at it that he appeared on NBC's *Dateline*. He became known as an expert on what it takes to arrest killers who thought they had gotten away with murder.

In his job, Detective Wallace was a skeptic. "As a cop, if you believe everything people tell you, then you'd never arrest anyone," he said. For him, facts need to be solid. Witnesses have to be believable. Evidence must be persuasive. Corroboration is always crucial. And alibis have to be proven.

In terms of religion, Detective Wallace was a skeptic too. At least until he was thirty-five. Then he started looking at the New Testament the way a detective would look at a case, including "forensic statement analysis." This skill involves analyzing a person's account of events—including word choice and structure—to find out if he is telling the truth or not.

Wallace did a six-month investigation, marking up the gospels in three Bibles to cross-check and verify each statement the writers made. His verdict? "The gospels reliably recorded true events. But that presented a problem for me," he said, "because they talk about the resurrection and other miracles. I could believe [them] if they said

Jesus ate bread, but what if they said the loaf levitated? C'mon, I couldn't believe that. I didn't believe miracles could happen, so I rejected them out of hand."

Eventually, what convinced Wallace miracles were possible was science. "I asked myself, *Do I believe* anything *supernatural?* And I concluded that, well, yes, even as an atheist, I did believe that something extra-natural occurred."

That thing was the big bang. "I realized that if there was something extra-natural that caused the beginning of all space, time, and matter as recorded in Genesis 1:1, then that same cause could accomplish all the miracles recorded in the gospels. In other words, if there is a God, then miracles are reasonable, even expected."

With that, Wallace was convinced that Christianity is true beyond a reasonable doubt, and went on to earn a master's degree in theological studies. He's now an adjunct professor of apologetics at Biola University.

Who better to ask about a two-thousand-year-old cold case?

Did Jesus Really Die on the Cross?

Even if we agree the gospels are rooted in eye-witness testimony—which Wallace spent six months investigating—there's still the issue of whether the resurrection, one of the greatest miracles ever, makes sense. And "solving" the case of Jesus' death is important, because if Jesus didn't rise from the dead, nothing in the gospels matters. But if there's going to be a miracle resurrection, somebody has to be dead. So an important question is this: Did Jesus really die on the cross? In recent years, opponents to Christianity have been trying to cast doubts.

As a result, I needed a homicide detective's input on some arguments I have heard.

1. Is it reasonable that Jesus would die as soon as the Bible says he did? The thieves on either side of him were still alive. Why wouldn't Jesus be?

Wallace said there's an important detail to remember. "The path to the cross for Jesus was dramatically different than the path for the thieves."

Wallace continued. "Pilate didn't want to crucify Jesus like the crowd was demanding, so he kind of makes an offer. He says, in effect, 'I'll tell you what I'll do—I'll beat him to within an inch of his life. Will that satisfy you?' Consequently, Jesus was given an especially horrific flogging. That didn't satisfy the crowds, and Jesus was crucified. But he was already in such extremely bad shape that he couldn't even carry his cross."

It makes sense that he would die sooner than men who hadn't been beaten as severely.

2. Were the soldiers wrong when they thought Jesus had died? Maybe Jesus was still alive when they took him down from the cross. After all, the soldiers weren't trained medical doctors. Could they have been mistaken?

"That objection usually comes from people who've never been around dead bodies," Wallace told me. "As a cop, I've witnessed a lot of autopsies. Let me tell you: dead people aren't like corpses in movies. They look different. They feel different. They get cold; they get stiff; their blood pools. These soldiers knew what death looked like."

In fact, Wallace pointed out, the soldiers had a good reason to make sure Jesus was dead: they would be executed themselves if a prisoner escaped alive!

There is also a medical clue in the apostle John's description of Jesus' death. As Wallace said, "[John] says when Jesus was stabbed with a spear to make sure he was dead, water and blood came out. In those days, nobody understood that. Some early church leaders thought this was a metaphor for baptism or something. Today, we know this [makes medical sense], because the torture would have caused fluid to collect around his heart and lungs.

"And," Wallace added, "we have no record of anyone ever surviving a full Roman crucifixion."

3. Was the person who died on the cross really Jesus? Maybe God supernaturally switched people on the cross. According to the Qur'an, it wasn't Jesus who died on the cross. It was someone "made to resemble him." Many Muslims believe God substituted Judas for Jesus on the cross.

"Here's one problem," Wallace said. "[The Qur'an] was written six hundred years after Jesus lived. Compare that to the first-century sources that are uniform in reporting that Jesus was dead. Not only do we have the gospel accounts, but we also have five ancient sources *outside* the Bible."

And there's another problem with the supernatural switch idea. "That would mean Jesus was being deceptive when he appeared to people afterward. That would contradict what we know about his character. And how would you explain him showing the nail holes in his hands and the wound in his side to Thomas?"

In Wallace's expert opinion, the evidence is clear: Jesus did die on the cross.

Was Jesus Really Buried?

Some people suggest that Jesus wasn't buried. That would explain why the tomb was empty on Easter morning.

A professor and author named Bart Ehrman recently wrote a book saying it's unlikely that Jesus was buried in a tomb. He argues that a criminal's body would be left to rot and be eaten by animals.

Other experts disagree. Craig Evans, a leading New

Testament scholar, pointed out that the Romans permitted Jewish customs during peacetime, and it was Jewish custom to bury a body. A Jewish archaeologist named Jodi Magness says that the gospel accounts of Jesus' burial "are consistent with archaeological evidence and with Jewish law."[28]

"I'll add one thing," Wallace said to me. "An ossuary (casket) with the remains of a crucifixion victim was discovered in 1968 with part of an iron spike still in his heel bone. This is evidence that at least some crucifixion victims were buried, as the earliest account of Jesus' death tells us he was."

Did Jesus Really Come Back from the Dead?

Whatever occurred two thousand years ago, it's clear that the disciples said that the once-dead Jesus appeared to them alive. Not only do the four gospels report this, but there's confirmation from students of the apostles (Clement and Polycarp), as well as an early creed of the church found in 1 Corinthians 15 and a speech by Peter in Acts 2.

Again, I wanted a detective's professional opinion on the case.

1. Were the eyewitnesses lying? "You've broken a lot of conspiracy cases as a cop," I said to Wallace. "Do you see any way these people could have been lying about this?"

He briefly outlined for me what you need for a successful conspiracy, and compared it with the witness to the resurrection.

- A small number of coconspirators. But more than five hundred people saw the risen Jesus at the same time (1 Corinthians 15:6).
- A short amount of time to keep up the lie. But the account of Jesus' resurrection has been told for over two thousand years without being disproved!
- Excellent communication between the coconspirators so they can make sure their stories line up. Suppose those five hundred people were lying. Now imagine that an outsider asked one of them, "What did Jesus say to the five hundred of you?" Lying guy makes something up. Then he needs to tell the other 499 people what he said, before the outsider can ask any one of them. He can't phone them, obviously. He can try to talk to everyone face to face, or maybe send a messenger. But he doesn't know who the outsider might talk to first. There's no way lying guy can get to all 499 coconspirators in time.
- Little or no pressure applied to those who are telling the lie. But we know that Christians were persecuted and even died for their belief in the risen Christ.

Wallace has experience interrogating witnesses. He says, "My experience is that people aren't willing to suffer or die for what they know is a lie." The witnesses to the risen Jesus knew the truth about what happened. And they were willing to stake their lives on it.

2. Were the eyewitnesses mistaken? "I'm sure you've seen cases where people close to a murder victim are so full of grief that it colors their memory about what happened," I said.

"To some degree," Wallace replied. "But I sense where you're going with this: Did sorrow cause people to have a vision of the risen Jesus? That's a different matter altogether."

He listed these problems with the theory:

- First, groups don't have hallucinations. But the earliest report of the resurrection said five hundred people saw Jesus at once.
- Second, different groups of people saw Jesus at different times and different places. The vision theory doesn't seem likely in those varying circumstances.
- Third, at least one person who saw Jesus *wasn't* swayed by wishful thinking. The last thing Paul wanted was evidence that Jesus was alive. But he saw the risen Jesus anyway!

3. Were the eyewitnesses fooled? It doesn't seem believable that over five hundred people had the same hallucination. But what if just one person did?

"What if one of the disciples—maybe Peter—experienced a vision due to his sorrow and then convinced others that Jesus had returned?" I asked the detective. "As you know, Peter had a strong personality and could be persuasive."

"I've had murder cases where one emphatic witness persuaded others that something happened," Wallace agreed. "The persuader has all the details in their most robust (strongest) form, while the others tend to generalize because they didn't actually see the event for themselves. But this theory can't account for the numerous, divergent, and separate group sightings of Jesus, which were described with a lot of specificity. Also, Peter wasn't the first to see the risen Jesus."

Why Don't Jews Accept the Resurrection?

Most of the eyewitnesses who saw the risen Jesus were Jewish. So why don't more Jewish people today accept the resurrection?

Most people would probably say that they have rational reasons for not believing that Jesus rose from the dead. But it is possible that many Jewish people have not looked seriously at the claims of the Christian faith. If they did, I wonder whether they would be like my Jewish friends who took the time to research the issues for themselves and came to faith in Christ.

Louis Lapides, for example, explored the ancient prophecies about the Messiah in the Jewish scriptures. And he discovered that Jesus fulfilled those prophecies against all odds.

The late Stan Telchin set out to expose the "cult" of Christianity after his daughter went away to college and received *Yeshua* (Jesus) as her Messiah. His investigation led him and his wife to the resurrected Jesus. Stan later became a pastor.

There's also an emotional reason to reject the resurrection. In Jewish families, there are barriers of culture and tradition. Christians see Jesus as the fulfillment of Jewish prophecies. But when a Jewish person comes to faith in Christ, their families may see it as a betrayal of their Jewish identity. Would you dare risk that kind of family conflict?

The Jewish people are very concerned with following God's laws. In fact, over the years, religious leaders added six hundred more laws to the commands already in the Jewish scriptures. Good Jews try to be obedient to God's laws.

As Wallace put it, "It can be hard to accept a grace-based system that says, 'The laws were there to show that you need for forgiveness. You can never totally obey them all.' A lot of people don't want to accept that."

The truth is, though, that accepting the miracle of the resurrection can lead to a second miracle that is just as amazing. When we exchanged our sin for God's grace, we become "new creations" (2 Corinthians 5:17).

A Personal Miracle

When that happened to then-Detective Wallace, he was changed in ways that couldn't be explained in mere human terms.

He told me, "Being a cop had led me to lose faith in people. My heart had shriveled. To me, everyone was a liar. Everyone was capable of depraved behavior. I saw myself as superior to everyone else. I was cynical, cocky, and distant."

Honestly, I was surprised by his description of himself. I have only known him as a warm, sincere, and generous person—but then, I have only known him since he has been a follower of Jesus.

"It sounds like a cliché," Wallace continued, "but coming to faith in Christ changed me drastically over time. As someone forgiven much, I learned to forgive others. After receiving God's grace, I was better able to show compassion. Now my life is consumed with letting others know that faith in Christ isn't just a subjective emotion. It's grounded in the truth of the resurrection."

That's the lasting power of the miracle of the resurrection. I see it over and over. It's true in my own experience and in the experience of countless others. The resurrection miracle brings personal miracles of forgiveness, redemption, and new life.

PART 3

Difficulties with
MIRACLES

CHAPTER 7

———•———

EMBARRASSED BY THE SUPERNATURAL

Have you ever felt embarrassed about talking about something God did in your life?

I have.

I was in a conference room, surrounded by my pastor, several of the church's elders, and a college professor of theology. They were interviewing me for ordination as a minister. I had left my journalism career and joined the staff of a large church in suburban Chicago. Being ordained was a next step.

I had no problem sharing the story of how I went from being an atheist to being a committed follower of Jesus. I had used my journalism and legal training to investigate the scientific and historical evidence for Christianity. I knew that would make sense to the people in the room. They would certainly relate to how God used logic and reason to lead me.

But I was wrestling with how much I should tell about the rest of my story. Should I mention the dream I had as a kid, when an angel appeared to me and gave me a prophecy that came true sixteen years later? What would they think if I described something supernatural like that?

Of course, everyone in the room believed in a miracle-working God. Still, would they think less of me if I began chattering about dreams and angels and personal prophecies? Is that a step too far? Would mouths fall open if I made the claim that my dream was an actual encounter with a messenger from the Almighty? Where is the line between sheer irrationality and a reasonable belief that God has intervened miraculously in my life?

In the end, I did tell them about the dream with the angel—and no one thought I was weird. And they ordained me as a pastor. But I have always remembered how uncomfortable I felt about sharing that part of my story. In fact, to this day I almost never refer to the dream in public.

That's why I was interested when I saw a blog post titled, "Embarrassed by the Supernatural." Without even reading it, I could relate. In America today, even Christians like me often hesitate to talk openly about divine interventions in our lives.

We don't want to be seen as weird. We don't want to be lumped with TV preachers or phony faith healers. We want to be respectable and accepted by people in our secular culture. The result? In our churches and even in our prayers, sometimes we hold back from fully embracing the God who still performs miracles.

I noticed that the author of the blog was a professor at Baylor University, just a few hours from my home. I decided to go talk with him.

Expecting the Ordinary

Professor Roger Olson has been part of churches from a variety of denominations. He has been a Pentecostal, a Presbyterian, and a Baptist. So he is able to talk about different kinds of churches from experience, as well as from his studies.

We discussed the idea that some churches today act as if God isn't present—planning things without thinking biblically, not trusting that God can and will provide for the congregation if they're following his will, or truly believing God is a part of our world and our lives.

"The situation varies from one denomination to another," Professor Olson told me. "But I agree that American religion in general has become secularized. That is, a lot of churches don't really believe that God intervenes or guides, except through what we might call human wisdom and reason. The truth is, they don't really expect God to do anything except in their interior (personal) spiritual lives."

"Can you give me an example?" I asked.

"We still hold on to the idea that God can change people, but mostly we mean God will help them turn over a new leaf, rather than a radical transformation. When that kind of radical rebirth does happen, we go, 'Wow! We didn't really know that could still occur! I wish it would happen more often.' But then we sink back into not really expecting it to occur again. After all, we don't want to get too fanatical."

"Still," I said, "balance is important."

"True. I've been in churches where the opposite attitude prevailed and people thought miracles were an everyday occurrence. Everything became a miracle. That's another danger too; it takes away the specialness. To me, the book of Acts is the best guide."

I mentally scrolled through Acts, which tells the story of the early church. The apostles seemed to go around expecting that when they told people about Jesus and his resurrection, something supernatural might very well happen. But that's not true today, Professor Olson said.

"All we expect to happen these days when we proclaim Jesus and the resurrection is that people will nicely nod and say, 'Oh, we agree with that.' Then they go home and live as if that's not really true, because they don't expect miracles to happen anymore. They don't expect God to do things that are inexplicable (baffling)."

"Why Are We Whispering?"

Whether they recognize it or not, many American Christians believe that miracles belong to the past (biblical times) and elsewhere (mission fields). They don't think of miracles as something that could happen in their lives.

"This is obvious from the way we react when someone gets sick," Professor Olson said. "Of course, we pray for them, but what do we ask? That God would comfort them in the midst of their suffering. That God would guide the hands of surgeons. That God would give doctors wisdom and discernment. What's missing?"

I answered, "Asking God to supernaturally heal them."

That's been true in my experience. Back in 2012, my wife, Leslie, found me unconscious on our bedroom floor. I was rushed by ambulance to the hospital. When I woke up, a doctor told me, "You're one step away from a coma, two steps away from dying."

I was suffering from severe hyponatremia—dangerously low blood sodium. It was causing my brain cells to absorb water and expand inside my skull. The prognosis if untreated: mental confusion, hallucinations, seizures, coma, and death.

While I received urgent treatment in the hospital, friends

came by to pray for me. Many of them did exactly as Professor Olson said: they prayed for wisdom for the physicians and for my strength—both of which I greatly appreciated—but very few came out and asked God, in a direct, bold, and straightforward way to supernaturally heal me.

Olson mentioned a pastor whose wife is a medical doctor.

"I was telling them about my own physical healing, even though I'm often reluctant to share that story. Then the pastor lowered his voice and said quietly, 'You know, my daughter was very sick, and I anointed her with oil and prayed fervently for her and she was healed—it was absolutely supernatural.' And I thought, *Why are we whispering?*"

I chuckled. "Seems like he should be shouting about this."

"Well," said Olson, "that illustrates the problem. Then he [admitted] to me that his church probably wouldn't respond favorably to his story."

No Modern Miracles?

Some Bible-believing theologians say that God no longer offers a spiritual gift of healing. Others say miracles themselves have ceased. They believe that once the Bible was written and the early church grew during the Roman Empire, miracles were no longer needed and so God stopped doing them.

Olson doesn't agree.

"My mother died of heart damage from rheumatic fever when I was two and a half years old," he told me. "At age ten, I contracted strep throat and was very, very sick. My family believed in God's healing through prayer, and doctors were a last resort, but they took me to a doctor who wrote a prescription for penicillin."

The penicillin might have cured young Roger Olsen's strep throat. But his stepmother threw the prescription away.

"She said, 'I don't think you really need this,'" Olson explained. "Well, a week later, I developed rheumatic fever, just like my mother. I was sick and in and out of hospitals for three months. Rheumatic fever attacks the valves of your heart. Most patients eventually need heart-valve replacement surgery. That didn't exist when my mother died."

Young Roger developed a heart murmur as a result of his illness. The elders of the church went to the Olson house. They anointed young Roger with oil and prayed for him. Later, Roger went for his weekly checkup. The doctor said, "I don't hear any heart murmur. And your blood test for inflammation is normal."

Today, Roger Olson has zero heart-valve damage. He goes to the cardiologist every year to check. The cardiologist always says the same thing: "You don't have a rheumatic heart."

"Still, it's scary to think of your stepmother throwing away the prescription for the antibiotic that could have prevented the rheumatic fever in the first place," I said.

"I don't think it's the best approach to say, 'God will heal me, so I'm just going to pray,'" Olson agreed. "Usually God works through natural means. He expects us to make use of the gifts he has provided to us, such as medication and technology. Otherwise, it would be like expecting manna to fall from heaven when there's a grocery store down the block."

I smiled. "That's a good analogy."

"The best approach," he concluded, "is to merge both prayer and medicine."

The Pentecostal church the Olsons attended had no problem accepting young Roger Olson's healing as a miraculous gift from God. For them, the supernatural was an ever-present element in their lives.

Olson remembers when a little boy from the church accidently opened the door and fell out of the family car while it was going down the road. When his parents rushed to pick him up, they thought he would be dead. But instead, he was just standing there. They said, "What happened?" He said, "Well, didn't you see the man? He caught me."

Some Christians may believe that miracles happened only in Bible times. Professor Olson is not one of them.

Mission-Field Miracles

Some people say that God no longer does miracles in places like the US. They admit he does still do miracles in Africa and other places in the Third World, because that's the leading edge of the gospel.

Does that explain why so many American Christians have never experienced a miracle? Has God just stopped doing them here?

We've already seen that there truly are areas of the world where God seems to be working especially strongly through miracles. (See chapters 2 and 3.) But Olson warned against assuming that God is done with miracles in the US.

"We need the supernatural as much as they do in China," he insisted. "America is still a mission field. I suspect that real Christianity is a minority, even among people who call themselves Christian. Too often, we think we only need apologetics, evidence, debates, and arguments to spread the gospel here rather than to see God do a supernatural work."

Professor Olson's classes at Baylor attract students from around the globe, including Third World countries where Christianity and its attitude toward the supernatural look quite different than in the United States.

When these African and Asian students see Western evangelicalism for the first time, Professor Olson told me,

"They say, 'This is not our Christianity. Our Christianity in Africa is surrounded by spiritual warfare. We can't brush it off as superstition. God really intervenes and does amazing things, but we don't see that here.'"

Why not? These students say, "We think it's your prosperity, individualism, materialism, and a lack of belief in the spiritual world."

Olson agrees. "In fact," he said, "I [can] almost predict by the brand of cars in the parking lot what the church believes. The more prosperous and educated we are, the more likely we are to substitute our own cleverness and accomplishments for the power of prayer. That's the seductive power of prosperity—it makes us less reliant on God. We think we've got everything under control." He went on to say, "The richer we get, the more education we attain, the less comfortable we are with the miraculous. We don't feel we need it, really. We're getting along just fine. After all, we're successful."

Then he added an observation I really related to. "Many [Christians] don't really believe in the supernatural until the doctor says, 'You have a terminal illness.'"

I can remember lying in my hospital bed when the doctor told me that I could be facing death. I suddenly felt desperate and dependent on God to rescue me. No question about it; times like that strip away our self-sufficiency and leave us frantic for God's direct supernatural touch.

"Before an experience like that," Olson continued, "many people don't make room in their life for God to do anything supernatural. Oh, sure, they believe in God; they love Jesus. But he's an image much more than a living reality."

Fear of Failure—God's Failure

Once when I was a young staff member at Willow Creek Church, I had to fill in for a pastor at a prayer meeting. The prayers were for people seeking healing from God. About a hundred people gathered in our chapel as we put James 5:14 into practice: "Is anyone among you sick? Let them call the elders of the church to pray over them and anoint them with oil in the name of the Lord."

My role would be to offer a general prayer on behalf of everyone there. For those who then wanted individual prayer and anointing, several of our elders were on hand afterward.

I have to confess that I felt conflicted. Much of the prayer came easily—asking for God to provide wisdom to the physicians, to comfort those who were suffering, to relieve pain, to strengthen hope and faith, to guide the hands of surgeons, and so forth. All of that, of course, was important.

But when it came to specifically asking God for

healing, how bold should I be? How strongly should I phrase my request? My secret fear: *What if I stuck out my neck and asked God for healing—and nothing happened?* Was I copping out when I concluded my prayer with, "Your will be done"?

Ultimately, I prayed as authentically as I could. I did ask God to supernaturally restore the health of all those gathered. But in the back of my mind, I wondered if he would really come through for them in this world. Selfishly, I fretted that my own reputation was at stake.

After all, for every miracle like the one that happened to Professor Olson as a child, there are many others whose healing won't come until heaven.

"Maybe that's a reason why our churches don't pursue those prayers—they don't want to be embarrassed if an answer doesn't come. How do we explain it when God *doesn't* heal someone?" I asked Professor Olson.

"We don't," came his response. "I believe God is sovereign and not arbitrary. He knows what he's doing. When he doesn't answer our prayers as we want, there may be particularities about the situation that we just don't understand."

I'm not saying that when God doesn't heal someone, you should look for the reason. For instance, it's common in some churches to blame the patients' lack of faith if God doesn't heal them.

That's simply harmful. We have to move away from trying to explain why a particular individual wasn't healed. That's God's business. All we know is that he asked us to pray for their healing, and we have to be obedient.

And if the person we were praying for thinks God failed? Well, we have to trust that God can deal with that too.

Gentle Whispers of God

Not all miracles are spectacular healings. Not every supernatural act is as earth-shattering as someone rising from the dead. More often, God speaks in gentle whispers. Or he directs everyday events in a way that sends a message of encouragement or hope to someone who needs it.

Many Christians experience these subtle "leadings" or "impressions" from God. But they're often reluctant to talk about them for fear of the skeptical reaction they'll receive. And so they keep quiet, embarrassed by the supernatural.

My friend Bill Hybels, the leader of Willow Creek Community Church, says, "When I make public reference to the whispers of God, I barely make it off the stage before half a dozen people approach to remind me that ax murderers often defend their homicides by claiming, 'God told me to do it.'"

Yet Hybels has found that these subtle but very real

communications from God have redirected his path. They have rescued him from temptations and reenergized him during some of his deepest moments of despair.

I asked Professor Olson for his opinion about whether God still speaks to his followers.

"No question," he said with little hesitation. "I continue to believe God speaks to his people today."

In one of his blog posts, Olson described how he walked away from a medical examination deeply troubled and discouraged. The doctor had found a problem, and surgery might be required.

The next day, an old hymn began running through Olson's mind, even though he hadn't heard the song since childhood. The words kept playing over and over, like a broken record, serving as background music all week.

"It's a hymn of comfort and assurance—of God's presence whatever happens," he said. "I simply thought it was my own mind's way of handling the emotional distress I was experiencing."

That Sunday, Olson went to his wife's church, where he noticed that the first hymn to be sung was #220, which was "Crown Him with Many Crowns." He reached for the hymnal from the rack in front of him and turned to #220—but that wasn't the song he found there. Instead, he found the hymn that had been running through his mind all week.

"Then I noticed that the hymnal I grabbed was not the church's hymnal, which doesn't even contain that hymn," he wrote. "It even had a different church's name embossed in gold letters on the front. I have never seen that hymnal before; it didn't belong there. I have no idea how it got there."

Indeed, it was the only one of those hymnals in the sanctuary—and it just happened to be in the rack directly in front of where Olson sat down.

"So what to make of that?" Olson asked. "Sheer coincidence? Possibly. Is it simply magical thinking to believe this was God sending me a message that the hymn was from him? Possibly. Half of me says, 'It's just a coincidence; don't make more of it.' The other half says, 'That's unbelief; accept it as from God.'"

Often Christians are nervous about these "God things." People have claimed to hear some pretty crazy and dangerous things from God. It's important to remember that nudgings from God today do not have the same inspiration and authority as Scripture. Everything must be tested against the Bible.

But like Olson, Hybels, and many others, I believe God does do "God things" today—even to the point of sending an angel in a dream to assure a spiritually confused kid that someday he would understand God's amazing grace.

That's something to celebrate, not to feel embarrassed about.

CHAPTER 8

•———•

WHEN MIRACLES
DON'T HAPPEN

Every day my wife, Leslie, is in pain. When traditional medical treatments failed, she tried acupuncture, deep massage, diet supplements, and other alternative therapies. While some brought temporary relief, none of them stopped the chronic muscle throbbing that assaults her over and over again.

Fibromyalgia affects the way the body processes pain signals. There is no known cure for it. And so year after year, decade after decade, Leslie copes as best she can with the discomfort, the soreness, the aching.

Let me tell you something else about Leslie: she is a wholly devoted follower of Jesus. She is a woman of spiritual depth whose persistent prayer was, in my view, the most influential factor in bringing me to faith in Christ. She devours the Bible daily. Her compassion for the hurting and spiritually confused is boundless. She is simply the finest and most devout person I have ever known.

Have we prayed for relief from her pain? *Continually.* Have we begged God for her healing? *Often and fervently.* Have we seen any improvement? *Quite the opposite.*

Could I give you half a dozen theological reasons why there's suffering in this sin-scarred world? Absolutely. I even give lectures on that topic. But this is *my* Leslie. This is *my* wife. This is *her* pain and suffering. And that makes this very personal.

While researching this book, I came across inspiring examples of how God miraculously restored sight to the blind, hearing to the deaf, and life to the dead. I celebrated each tangible expression of God's grace.

But after I wrote each story, I asked, *Why no miracle for Leslie?* Yes, I know God promises to cause good to come from our suffering if we're devoted to him. *But why no miracle for Leslie?* Yes, I understand that suffering produces perseverance and sharpens our character. *But why no miracle for Leslie?* Yes, I am aware that there will be no more tears in heaven. *But why no miracle for Leslie?* Every day, my wife is in pain. She needs a miracle.

The Miracle That Didn't Happen

Sometimes tragedy reawakens faith. Pain, as C. S. Lewis observed, can be God's megaphone to rouse the spiritually deaf. But what happens when, instead of a miraculous answer to prayer, we hear only silence from above? The miracle that doesn't happen can lead faith to shrink to nothing.

That's what happened to Michael Shermer, the editor of *Skeptic* magazine, who we met in chapter 1.

You see, Michael Shermer once lived as a Christian.

He met his girlfriend Maureen when they were both in college. They were still dating after Michael finished grad school. Maureen worked for an inventory firm, and she and her coworkers would drive in the middle of the night to a company and take inventory while it was closed. One night in the middle of nowhere, the van veered off the highway and rolled over several times. Maureen didn't have her seat belt on, and she broke her back.

She called Michael at about five in the morning. He asked, "What's going on?"

She said, "I'm in the hospital."

Michael was stunned, because she sounded normal. "What? What happened?"

She said, "I don't know. I can't move."

Maureen was paralyzed from the waist down.

During an all-nighter in the emergency room, Michael prayed. At that point in his life, he had pretty much checked out of the faith he'd had as a teenager. Still, he got on his knees and bowed his head.

"I was as sincere as I had ever been," he told me. "I asked God to overlook my doubts for the sake of Maureen, to heal her, to breathe life into her. As best I could at that moment, I believed. I *wanted* to believe. If there were a God who was powerful and loving, if there were any justice at all anywhere in the universe, then surely he'd help this precious, caring, compassionate young woman."

I waited for Shermer to continue. For a moment, there was silence. Then I asked, "What happened?"

He shook his head. "Nothing."

I let the word hang in the air before finally asking: "How did you react?"

He shrugged. "I wasn't very surprised. I thought, *Well, there probably is no God. Stuff just happens. ...* That's the way the world is."

"Was this the final nail in the coffin of your faith?"

"Yeah, that pretty much did it. I was like, 'Ah, the heck with it.'"

"Were you angry at God?"

"Nothing to be angry at. He's not there. This is just what happens. The good, the bad—it's pretty random."

I can understand why Michael felt that way. Maybe you can too. Maybe you've been begging God to meet an urgent need in your life—and no miracle is coming.

This chapter is for you—and Leslie and Michael. And me.

Becky's Story

Sometimes Leslie experiences "fibro fog," a mental cloudiness or forgetfulness that comes with her illness. That's what my friend Douglas Groothuis thought was happening with his wife, Becky, who had been diagnosed with fibromyalgia several years earlier.

Then one day, she went to the same hair salon where she had been going for years—but she couldn't find her way home. Becky was missing for several hours; Doug finally had to call the police. Clearly, this was more than simple absentmindedness.

Becky was diagnosed with a progressive, incurable, and fatal brain disease. Humanly speaking, there is no hope. Death is as certain as the slow loss of her ability to speak, to think, to plan, and to perform the simplest of tasks. As committed Christians, Doug and Becky have earnestly prayed for God's help—and yet, all the while, she continues to gradually lose her mind.

Doug and Becky were in their late twenties when they met. She was a writer and editor, and he was a campus minister.

"She was an elegant writer and a sharp editor," Doug told me. "She always improved what I wrote."

"What did she add?"

"Clarity. The perfect word. The right turn of a phrase.

She loved language. She could write magnificent sentences that flowed for sixty words or more."

Doug and Becky were married a year after they met. Becky was in her thirties when she was diagnosed with fibromyalgia. "It was a fairly new diagnosis back then—some doctors didn't know what to make of it," Doug said. "We tried alternate therapies, but nothing helped very much."

I had gone through the same process with Leslie, starting in the days when skeptical doctors thought the illness was more psychological than physical.

"Over time," Doug told me, "she began experiencing forgetfulness and confusion. At that point, we didn't know if it was the early stages of dementia or what. The most troubling event was when she went to the hair salon—which she had visited dozens of times—and couldn't find her way home. I had to file a missing person report with the police. It was a horrible evening."

The forgetfulness kept getting worse.

"She went to the dentist and when she got in the car afterward, she didn't know how to start it. I went and found that the car had been in gear," Doug said. "She once asked me, 'How do you work the windshield wipers on our car?' At that point, we had owned that car for ten years. She had increasing difficulty working on the computer—in fact, I bought her a new one that was simpler to use, but she never figured it out. I ended up giving it away."

Sliding into Dementia

Then the day after Valentine's Day in 2014, Doug rushed Becky to the emergency room for acute depression.

"She basically couldn't get out of bed. She couldn't talk," he said. "The psychiatrist put her in the behavioral health unit of a hospital across town. They strapped her down and took her away on a stretcher—she looked so forlorn."

Becky was hospitalized for five weeks. "I visited her virtually every day. It was incredibly sad to see her in that psychiatric unit, wandering aimlessly, muddled and confused. At the end, she wasn't even able to sign the release papers. They diagnosed her with primary progressive aphasia."

Primary progressive aphasia is a pretty rare disease. *Aphasia* is a difficulty finding words, especially nouns. This is especially sad because Becky loved language so much.

"Just this morning," Doug told me, "she came downstairs upset because she couldn't find a hairbrush and she couldn't think of the word for it. She would gesture and point to her hair. I said, 'Hairbrush?' She said, 'Yes.' The other day she didn't know what the telephone was or how to work it."

Doug continued. "I always marveled at Becky's mind. She was smarter than I am. I remember cleaning out some papers and finding her membership card from Mensa, the society for certified geniuses. I held it—and I cried. Her signature at the bottom was in her beautiful handwriting—but today, she can't write a word. She doesn't know how to use a pen."

"We live in a disposable society, where divorce is common," I said. "Yet you have stayed married."

Doug smiled. "The decision to stay married and be supportive of my wife was settled when we exchanged our wedding vows—for better, for worse, in sickness and in health. Of course, that turned out to be more profound than either of us thought."

Hope on Hold

Patients with primary progressive aphasia lose their use of words and then their executive functions—the ability to analyze and perform tasks. The particular cruelty of this disease is that Becky is slowly losing her mind—and she's aware of it slipping away.

"When Becky despairs, what do you say to her?" I asked Doug.

"What can I say? I can't tell her it's going to get better in this life. That wouldn't be honest, and we're committed to avoiding clichés and too-easy answers," he replied.

"So I tell her to take it one day at a time, to look for the good things in life, to remember that God loves her. I say, 'Think of the future, of the world without tears, without a curse, when you'll have a perfect resurrection body and you'll be face-to-face with God.'"

"Does that help her?"

"It does. In fact, just this morning, I said to her, 'In the long run, everything will be all right.' She asked, 'What do you mean?' I said, 'The new heaven and the new earth.'"

"How did she respond?"

"Big smile. We have hope, but it's deferred," he replied. "Recently Becky and I were having dinner, and I felt moved to offer a toast."

"A toast?" I said. "To what?"

"To the source of our hope," he said. "To the afterlife."

Inscrutable Suffering

Having hope doesn't take away all of today's pain, of course. Doug told me, "I'm becoming an expert on suffering." With a weak smile, he added, "I wish God had picked someone else."

How do you keep trusting a God who is all good and all-powerful and still allows so much suffering?

For Doug, the answer is in the big picture.

"Christianity has the best explanation for evil and

suffering because of the fall of humanity," he said. "Ever since then, the world has been plagued by death, decay, and disappointment. But because Christ experienced the worst of the world and triumphed over it and is now at the right hand of the Father, I know there will be a resurrection, and my wife and I will live in the new heaven and the new earth. Granted, God has not dealt with suffering and evil completely, but we have the assurance that he *will*."

Then Doug said something I didn't expect. "You see, there's a difference between meaningless suffering and inscrutable suffering."

The word *inscrutable* means "impossible to understand." I wasn't sure how that could be comforting. So Doug explained.

"*Meaningless suffering* means that suffering is simply there. It doesn't achieve a greater good. It has no purpose. *Inscrutable suffering* means we don't know what the purpose is, but we have reason to believe that God is providential, loving, and all-powerful. Our suffering may seem meaningless to us, but it's not.

"Here's the point: God uses evil to produce a greater good that could not be achieved otherwise—though we may not understand how. God is unlimited in power and knowledge and wisdom, and we are not. We should expect that certain things will be [beyond our understanding]."

A philosopher once told me that if God can take the very worst thing that could ever happen in the universe—the death of his Son on a cross—and turn it into the very best thing ever to happen in the universe—the opening of heaven for all who follow him—then he is able to take our difficult circumstances and draw good from them.[29]

Before we'd started talking about Becky, I'd asked Doug for his thoughts on that.

"There's truth to that," he answered. "I often go back to Genesis 50:20, where Joseph says to his brothers who betrayed him, 'You intended to harm me, but God intended it for good.' We may not know what good God is achieving in the short run, but given the credibility of Christianity and my forty years of experience as a Christian, I am justified in believing that there can be significance and purpose in suffering."

"Yet," I said, "often that's small comfort when we're in pain."

"We can't read the mind of God," came his reply. "We [don't know] why he chooses to work a miracle in some cases and not others. Yes, it can be agonizing when you've prayed and fasted for the healing of a loved one and God seems to have said no or to wait until eternity."

Doug says it helps that he knows that Jesus understands what pain is like.

As we were discussing his experience since Becky

was diagnosed, he said, "When I'm angry at God, when I'm distressed and anguished and seething at my circumstances, I think of Christ hanging on the cross for me. This brings me back to spiritual sanity. He endured the torture of the crucifixion out of his love for me. He didn't have to do that. He chose to. So he doesn't just sympathize with us in our suffering; he empathizes with us. Ultimately, I find comfort in that."

The Prayer of Letting Go

"Do you still pray for a miracle?" I asked. "Do you continue to ask God to supernaturally heal Becky?"

"For a long time, we prayed and fasted and prayed some more. We sought out people who are gifted in healing. We read all the books on healing and tried to follow their advice. But these days, I only pray for a miracle every once in a while. Sometimes I come up behind Becky when she's eating and hug her. I touch her head and I ask, 'God, will you go in there and fix this?' Part of her brain is dying, and it's terrible. But, no, I don't pray for a miracle much anymore."

To be honest, that surprised me. "Then what do you pray for?"

"I pray for wisdom in dealing with all the complications of being a caretaker. I pray for her spiritual well-being and for ways to give her some meaning and happiness."

"So you've lost hope of a healing?" I asked.

"There's a verse in Ecclesiastes that says there's a time to give up. After we got the diagnosis, I didn't give up on God, I didn't give up on Becky, but after a while, I essentially gave up on her being healed."

"But shouldn't we *always* be praying for God's miraculous intervention?" I asked. "To give up seems . . ." I searched for the right word, not wanting to sound harsh. "Well, it seems a little . . . unspiritual."

To my relief, Doug wasn't offended. "Not at all," he said. "Remember, I'm not giving up on my faith. I'm not walking away from God. I'm not leaving Becky, and I'm not abandoning hope. But sometimes the most appropriate step when your pleas for healing aren't being answered is to pray a prayer of relinquishment." A prayer of letting go.

He explained. "At Gethsemane, Jesus asked the Father to rescue him from the fate of the cross, but his final prayer was one of relinquishment. He surrendered when he could have escaped. He put himself totally in his Father's hands—whatever his Father had in store for him was what he wanted for himself. And when healing isn't coming, sometimes we have to say, 'Lord, whatever you have in store for me is what I want,' as difficult as that might be at the time. In a sense, it's a prayer of obedience, of submission, of trust, of faith."

I asked, "How has praying a prayer of reliquishment changed your attitude toward healing?"

He reflected for a minute. "Rather than feeling like I'm always beating God with my fists," he said, "now I feel more like I'm resting in his arms."

When the Miracle Isn't Yours

By definition, miracles are outside the normal course of events. They're a supernatural exception to the way the world usually works. Though they're more common than we may think, they're still relatively rare—which means for most people, a sudden and complete healing isn't going to happen. But that doesn't mean God is absent. It doesn't imply that we face our struggles on our own.

The other day I came across a guest blog from someone who speaks with personal authority on miracles that haven't happened.

Tricia Lott Williford's husband died unexpectedly after being sick for less than a day. Suddenly, Tricia was a widowed single mom with two children under the age of five. She knows about personal heartache and unanswered prayers.

In the blog post I read, she shared some of her thoughts.[30]

"When God gives to other people in a way he hasn't given to you, it's easy to feel left out, and it's hard to want to hear how good he has been to other people," she writes.

So what do you do when you're in that situation?

In Tricia's experience, "Saying to God, 'Lord, I don't trust you, but I want to,' is the beginning of hope when the miracle isn't yours. This is the root of confidence even when God doesn't say yes. Ask him to show you where he is as he says no. He'll show you: he's with you."

Sometimes, that has to be enough.

REACHING YOUR VERDICT

I started this investigation to answer some questions. Does a miracle-performing God actually exist? And if so, is he still in the miracle business today? Is he available to intervene in *your* life? Or are modern-day "miracles" nothing more than coincidences, wishful thinking, and fraud?

Reaching My Verdict

As a looked into whether it's unscientific to believe in miracles, I quickly realized how important biases are. If you define miracles as breaking the unbreakable laws of nature, miracles are impossible. But if miracles are *temporary interventions* in the way the laws of nature usually work—well, that leaves room for science *and* miracles.

The STEP study that showed that prayer has no effect on healing isn't convincing to me. For one thing, the people doing the praying were part of a group that doesn't even believe in the possibility of divine intervention. It doesn't tell us anything about authentic Christian prayer on healing.

In addition, Candy Gunther Brown's research shows instant improvements in eyesight and hearing after hands-on prayer by sincere followers of Jesus. Other studies also show that prayer can have a positive impact on healing. More and more, researchers are finding that data support the case for miracles.

What's more, I found Craig Keener's study of miracles to be persuasive. I was impressed by so many examples of supernatural intervention in which there were multiple, reliable eyewitnesses, medical documentation, and no reasons for people to lie about it. I found myself agreeing that there might be other possible explanations for some of the miracle accounts, but not for all of them. Not by a long shot.

The extraordinary dreams among Muslims that missionary Tom Doyle told me about clearly go beyond mere coincidence. The dreamers met specific people that they had seen only in their dreams. That's not just happenstance; something peculiar was going on.

Something supernatural, you might say.

I found myself ever more convinced that the origin and fine-tuning of the universe, which physicist Michael

Strauss described, point powerfully toward the existence of a supernatural Creator.

And I am persuaded that the facts of history, cited by detective J. Warner Wallace, establish convincingly that Jesus of Nazareth not only claimed to be the unique Son of God, but he then proved it by returning from the dead.

In fact, the resurrection goes beyond confirming the existence of God and of miracles. The torture, death, and empty tomb of Christ also answer the question of *why* God would want to intervene in individual lives through his miraculous touch.

Jesus' willingness to endure the crucifixion tells us that God is motivated to take extraordinary action to rescue people. And if he loves people *that* much, then it's reasonable to believe there would be times when he would choose to use one hand to hold back the forces of nature, while he uses his other hand to miraculously heal someone who is suffering.

An Open Mind

It takes an open mind to consider the evidence for miracles. A lot of people have the attitude, "Miracles are impossible, period. Now, go ahead and try to make your case."

I get that. The Bible talks about our human tendency

to suppress the truth and walk the other way from God. I've seen that play out in my own life. When I was an atheist, I didn't *want* Christianity to be true. I was living an immoral, drunken, and selfish lifestyle—and I liked it.

When Leslie came to faith in Jesus, her character and values began to change for the better. While that was intriguing, I wanted the old Leslie back. I figured if I could disprove that Jesus returned from the dead, maybe I could debunk Christianity.

I knew I would be wasting my time if I approached the investigation with my conclusion already reached in advance. If my journalism training taught me anything, it was to keep an open mind as I pursued answers. At law school, I learned how to evaluate evidence and testimony to determine whether they are solid or shaky.

Here's what surprised me: Christianity *invites* investigation. When the gospels report supernatural events, they don't begin with, "Once upon a time . . ." Rather, they report specifics that can be checked out.

After nearly two years of research, I came to my own verdict about miracles: they're often credible and convincing, and they contribute to the larger case for Christ. Compelled by the facts, I joined Leslie in following Jesus—and the word *miracle* isn't far off in describing the way God has revolutionized my life as a result.

As for the time I invested in studying the evidence for

the book you're reading now, it was certainly well spent. In the end, my confidence in a miracle-working God has been deepened and strengthened. As a court of appeals would say, *The verdict is affirmed.*

Reaching Your Verdict

Now it's your turn. What is your verdict?

After reading this book, are you convinced that God continues to supernaturally intervene in people's lives? Or are you finding ways to explain away all the evidence that points to a miracle-working God who can act in your life? That's what I once did.

I'll never forget the day my newborn daughter was rushed into intensive care. She was clearly terribly ill, but none of the doctors could figure out the problem.

Even though I was an atheist at the time, I was so desperate that I actually prayed and begged God—if he existed—to heal her. Soon after that prayer, my daughter was completely back to normal health. The doctors didn't have any explanation.

My response was to explain it away as a coincidence. I wouldn't even consider the possibility that God had acted.

Even if there had been a hospital chart full of evidence of a miracle, I wouldn't have believed that God had answered my prayer. I had already made up my mind.[31]

You see, the issue wasn't whether I had enough evidence of a miracle-working God. The real issue was, Did I *want* to know God personally? Did I want to get free from guilt, to experience his power for daily living, to connect with him in this life and for eternity in the next?

Do you? As you reflect on the contents of this book, I trust that you will keep an open mind and a receptive heart.

God offers a free gift of forgiveness and eternal life to all who receive it in repentance and faith. That's what Jesus' death and resurrection were all about: paying the penalty we deserve for our failures and wrongdoing, and then rising to give us new life with him—forever.

That's the most valuable miracle of all.

And it's yours for the asking.

Notes

1. Anugrah Kumar, "Ben Carson Says God Helped Him Ace College Chemistry Exam by Giving Answers in a Dream," *Christian Post*, May 9, 2015, www.christianpost.com/news/ben-carson-says-God -helped-him-ace-college-chemisty-exam-by-giving -answers-in-dream-138913 (accessed October 30, 2017).

2. Helen Roseveare, *Living Faith* (Minneapolis, Bethany House, 1980), 44–45.

3. See Joel Landau, "'Mysterious Voice' Led Utah Cops to Discover Child Who Survived for 14 Hours in Submerged Car after Mom Drowned," *New York Daily News*, March 9, 2015, www.nydailynews.com/ news/national/mysterious-voice-leads-police-baby -car-crash-article-1.2142732 (accessed September 28, 2017); Leonard Greene, "Baby Survives Being Trapped 14 Hours in Submerged Car," *New York*

Post, March 9, 2015, nypost.com/2015/03/09/
baby-survives-14-hours-trapped-in-car-submerged
-in-icy-river (accessed September 28, 2017); Billy
Hollowell, "Police Can't Explain the Mysterious
Voice That They Claim Led Them to the Baby
Girl Trapped for 14 Hours in Frigid Waters,"
The Blaze, March 10, 2015, www.theblaze.com/
news/2015/03/10/police-cant-explain-the-mysterious
-voice-that-they-claim-led-them-to-the-baby-girl
-trapped-for-14-hours-in-frigid-waters (accessed
September 28, 2017).

4. See Craig S. Keener, *Miracles: The Credibility of New Testament Accounts* (Baker Books, 2011), 161–167.

5. Stephen Barr, "Has Science Subsumed the Miraculous?" part of essay series presented by John Templeton Foundation entitled "Are Miracles Possible?" published on Slate.com, undated. www .slate.com/bigideas/are-miracles-possible/essays-and -opinions/stephen-barr-opinion (accessed October 30, 2017).

6. Jerry A. Coyne, *Faith vs. Fact: Why Science and Religion Are Incompatible* (New York: Viking, 2015), 124.

7. Candy Gunther Brown, *Testing Prayer: Science and Healing* (Cambridge, MA: Harvard University Press, 2012), 7.

8. Quoting May Rowland, Silent Unity's director from 1916 to 1971; see Neal Vahle, *The Unity Movement: Its Evolution and Spiritual Teachings* (Philadelphia: Templeton Foundation Press, 2002), 246–47.

9. "What Is Affirmative Prayer?" www.unity.org/prayer/what-affirmative-prayer (accessed October 31, 2017), emphasis added.

10. Tim Stafford, *Miracles: A Journalist Looks at Modern-Day Experiences of God's Power* (Bloomington, MN: Bethany House, 2012), 150–51.

11. Rex Gardner, *Healing Miracles: A Doctor Investigates* (London: Darton, Longman & Todd, 1986), 202–5.

12. Genesis 18:25

13. See David McGee, "Christian Date of Adam from the Perspective of Young-Earth Creationism," answersingenesis.org/bible-characters/adam-and-eve/creation-date-of-adam-from-young-earth-creationism-perspective/, published November 28, 2012 (accessed 11/1/2017).

14. See article news.wgbh.org/post/big-bang-theory-roman-catholic-creation, published March 20, 2014 (accessed 11/1/2017).

15. See Domagoj Valjak, "The Big Bang theory of the universe was developed by a Catholic priest–and the Pope approved," www.thevintagenews.com/2017/09/27/the-big-bang-theory-of-the-universe-was

-developed-by-a-catholic-priest-and-the-pope
-approved/, published September 27, 2017 (accessed
11/1/2017).

16. From Patrick Cusworth, "Pope Francis's comments
on the Big Bang are not revolutionary. Catholic
teaching has long professed the likelihood of human
evolution," catholicherald.co.uk/commentandblogs/
2014/10/31/pope-franciss-comments-on-the-big
-bang-are-not-revolutionary-catholic-teaching-has
-long-professed-the-likelihood-of-human-evolution/,
published October 31, 2014 (accessed 11/1/2017).

17. See John Noble Wilford, "Primordial Helium,
Created in Big Bang, Detected at Long Last," *New
York Times*, June 13, 1995. www.nytimes.com/1995/
06/13/science/primordial-helium-created-in-big
-bang-detected-at-long-last.html?pagewanted=all
(accessed 11/6/2017).

18. See Calla Cofield, "Gravitational Waves: Ripples
in Spacetime," www.space.com/25088-gravitational
-waves.html, posted October 15, 2017 (accessed
11/6/2017).

19. William Lane Craig, *On Guard: Defending Your
Faith with Reason and Precision* (Colorado Springs:
David C. Cook, 2010), 74.

20. Paul Davies, *The Edge of Infinity* (New York: Simon
& Schuster, 1982), 90.

21. See Hugh Ross, *The Creator and the Cosmos: How the Greatest Scientific Discoveries of the Century Reveal God* (Colorado Springs: NavPress, 1995), 117.

22. Paul Davies, *The Cosmic Blueprint* (New York: Simon & Schuster, 1988), 203.

23. Edward Harrison, *Masks of the Universe: Changing Ideas on the Nature of the Universe* (New York: Macmillan, 1985), 252.

24. Quoted in Lee Strobel, *The Case for Faith* (Grand Rapids: Zondervan, 2000), 78.

25. Stephanie Margaret Bucklin, "Is the Multiverse Physics, Philosophy, or Something Else Entirely?" *Astronomy*, January 18, 2017. astronomy.com/news/2017/01/what-is-the-multiverse (accessed 11/7/2017).

26. Richard Swinburne, *Is There a God?* (Oxford: Oxford University Press, 1995), 68.

27. Quoted in Strobel, *Case for Faith*, 77.

28. Jodi Magness, "Jesus' Tomb: What Did It Look Like?" in *Where Christianity Was Born*, ed. Hershel Shanks (Washington, DC: Biblical Archaeology Society, 2006), 224.

29. See my interview with philosopher Peter Kreeft of Boston College in *The Case for Faith* (Grand Rapids: Zondervan, 2000), 30–54.

30. Tricia Lott Williford, "When Everyone Else Is Getting Their Miracle: How to Deal with Feeling

Overlooked," Ann Voskamp blog, July 10, 2017, www.annvoskamp.com/2017/07/when-everyone-else -is-getting-their-miracle-how-to-deal-with-feeling -overlooked (accessed November 7, 2017).

31. See *The Case for Faith*, 269.

Meet Lee Strobel

Atheist-turned-Christian Lee Strobel was an award-winning legal editor of *The Chicago Tribune*. He is a *New York Times* best-selling author of more than twenty books. He formerly taught First Amendment Law at Roosevelt University and currently serves as Professor of Christian Thought at Houston Baptist University.

Lee was educated at the University of Missouri (Bachelor of Journalism degree) and Yale Law School (Master of Studies in Law degree). He was a journalist for fourteen years at *The Chicago Tribune* and other newspapers, winning Illinois' highest honor for public service journalism from United Press International. He also led a team that won UPI's top award for investigative reporting in Illinois.

After examining the evidence for Jesus, Lee became a Christian in 1981. He became a teaching pastor at two churches and hosted the national network TV program *Faith Under Fire*. Now he is a teaching pastor at Woodlands Church in Texas.

Lee has won national awards for his books *The Case for Christ*, *The Case for Faith*, *The Case for a Creator*, and *The Case for Grace*. In 2017, his spiritual journey was depicted in a major motion picture, *The Case for Christ*, which ranks among the top twenty faith-based films at the box office.

Lee and Leslie have been married for forty-five years. Their daughter, Alison, is a novelist. Their son, Kyle, is a professor of spiritual theology at the Talbot School of Theology at Biola University.

The Case for Christ Student Edition

Lee Strobel with Jane Vogel

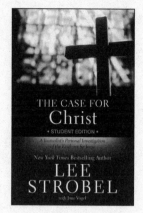

There's little question that Jesus actually lived. But miracles? Rising from the dead? Some of the stories you hear about him sound like just that—stories. A reasonable person would never believe them, let alone the claim that he's the only way to God! But a reasonable person would also make sure that he or she understood the facts before jumping to conclusions. That's why Lee Strobel—an award-winning legal journalist with a knack for asking tough questions—decided to investigate Jesus for himself. An atheist, Strobel felt certain his findings would bring Christianity's claims about Jesus tumbling down like a house of cards. He was in for the surprise of his life. Join him as he retraces his journey from skepticism to faith. You'll consult expert testimony as you sift through the truths that history, science, psychiatry, literature, and religion reveal. Like Strobel, you'll be amazed at the evidence—how much there is, how strong it is, and what it says. The facts are in. What will your verdict be in *The Case for Christ Student Edition*?

Available in stores and online!

ZONDERVAN®
.com

The Case for a Creator Student Edition

Lee Strobel with Jane Vogel

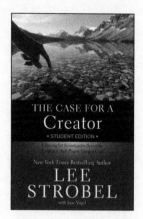

When Lee Strobel was a high school freshman, science convinced him that God didn't exist. Since then, however, incredible scientific discoveries have not only helped restore Lee's faith, but have strengthened it.

Lee is not alone. More and more scientists, confronted with startling, cutting-edge evidence from many areas of research, no longer believe the universe just "happened" or that life arose by mere chance. Behind a universe of staggering complexity, they are seeing signs of a Master Designer.

Are your science textbooks still telling you the same "facts" that Lee's did years ago? Prepare to be astonished by what some of today's most respected experts have to say about:

- The birth of the universe
- Darwinism and the origin of life
- The astounding fine-tuning of the cosmos
- Amazing molecular machines and DNA research

Weigh the evidence for yourself. Then consider this question: Could it be that the universe looks designed ... because it is?

Available in stores and online!

ZONDERVAN®
.com

The Case for Faith Student Edition

Lee Strobel with Jane Vogel

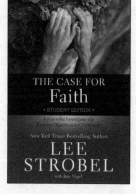

It's not easy to believe in Christianity when there is pain all around you and issues that defy easy explanation. Unless there are answers to the questions you face.

Lee Strobel knows how important it is to find answers that ring true. With his background as an award-winning journalist, asking tough questions has been his business. And while his search for the truth convinced Lee that Jesus is real, it also confronted him with some particularly knotty, gut-level questions about Christianity you've likely asked as well: *Why is there suffering? Doesn't science disprove miracles? What about hell—and the millions who've never heard of Jesus? Is God unjust?* They're the kinds of conundrums that can block— and have blocked—people's faith.

But those questions don't have to block yours. Join Lee in a fascinating journey of discovery. You'll gain powerful insights that will reshape your understanding of the Bible. And you'll read true stories about people whose experiences demonstrate that faith in Jesus not only makes excellent sense, it makes a life-changing difference as well.

Available in stores and online!

ZONDERVAN®
.com

The Case for the Real Jesus Student Edition

Lee Strobel with Jane Vogel

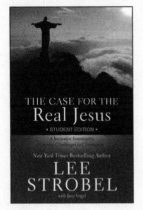

Was Jesus just a good man who lived a long time ago? Or was he something more?

Just about everyone you ask has an opinion about Jesus. Some believe he was the Son of God, while others question his existence altogether. Some believe he lived but that he was merely a good man. Today, scientists and other people are stating things that can make it difficult to know what to believe. So how can you know who the real Jesus was (and is)—especially when so many people are working to prove him to be a fake or a fraud? That's what Lee Strobel wanted to know.

As a former journalist—and a former atheist—Lee went on an investigative journey to discover the real Jesus, one that took him across the continent and into the homes of today's most prominent experts on Christian history. He found all the evidence he needed to believe that Jesus is indeed the Risen Savior.

Join Lee's investigation and discover the truth about Jesus for yourself. After you've seen all the evidence, you'll know for certain who the real Jesus is, and you'll be able to help others know him as well.

Available in stores and online!